GROWING CREATIVE CHILDREN

Marlene D. LeFever

Tyndale House
Publishers, Inc.,
Wheaton, Illinois

Library of Congress
Catalog Card Number
81-50140
ISBN 0-8423-1232-3, paper
Copyright © 1981
by Marlene D. LeFever
All rights reserved.
First printing,
September 1981
Printed in the
United States of America.

Dedicated to the people
in whose homes I lived as a child:

To my mother
who never had time to write creative ideas;
she lived them.

To my father
who knew that a shortcut down country roads
was always longer
but was also an invitation to adventure and fun.

To my Aunt Arro Doutrich
who told great stories
and never let being an adult
get in the way of laughter.

To my Uncle Lloyd Doutrich
who killed rattlesnakes,
took me on long bumpy trips into the groves
to find the world's biggest orange,
and taught me to make ugly,
wonderful shadow monsters.

CONTENTS

FOREWORD

I didn't buy my mother a balloon, and I've been sorry ever since. The lions were in the ring and the clowns were falling all over themselves. Popcorn, noise, roars: she and I loved the circus. All we two fully grown women needed to make our day perfect was a helium-filled balloon.

But seventy-five cents? We both remembered my growing-up years when our Friday nights were spent walking and talking through the downtown stores—with fifty cents between us. I just couldn't bring myself to splurge by paying almost a dollar for a balloon.

Too bad! Balloons belong in our homes and our relationships. And my mother filled my life with creative balloons. They weren't the circus ones that fly away or burst. They were, instead, the many experiences that helped mold and challenge my brother and me. If we were at the circus today, I would buy the biggest balloon I could find and present it to Mother. "Thanks for all the ideas, hours, and excitement," I'd say. "Thanks for the balloons with which you filled my childhood."

We had the only basement in town with a life-sized, motorized whale in it. I was with Mother the day she got it. She went into the supermarket and asked the manager what he was going to do with the big fish opening and shutting its mouth over the tuna display. "Don't toss it," Mother

begged. "It would make a great visual aid in the story of
Jonah." Mother was always looking for better ways to
communicate with children—my brother Jim and me, all
the neighborhood kids, and the thousands of children across
Lancaster County, Pennsylvania, who had been part of her
decades of Bible classes.

I don't think she ever thought, "How can I force my
kids to use all the creativity God gave them?" She just loved
doing fun things with us and watching in wonder when
one of us came up with something unexpected. "I'm so
proud of you," she would tell my brother after he built
one of his amazing creations in our basement. "No one else in
this family is the least bit mechanical." He would proudly
hold her verbal balloon, and the next time my father
announced that something couldn't be fixed, Jim would
fix it.

This book is filled with balloons. Some of them are my
mother's—given to my brother and me and passed on to
you. Many of the others were blown up and used by the
families who have invited me to be part of their lives.

Let these ideas be a starting point for creative planning
in your home. Some ideas may not be right for your
children. No one family could possibly get involved in all
the ideas here. Some ideas will need your creative adjustment
before they'll be just right for you. Others may be
tailor-made. Lift those off the page and into your living
room.

God gave us family—our own children and the children
who touch our lives. And in our busy days there are still
moments when it's perfect to say, "My child, let's create a
balloon together."

INTRODUCTION

Wouldn't it be wonderful if Christian parents always produced creative children?

God is the Creator. His purpose was to create people who could have communion with him, spirit to Spirit. We lost this communion when we sinned, but through Jesus' great creative act, his death and resurrection, this fellowship was again established. The Spirit of God dwells within us Christians and works through us. Since we are made in the image of God, with God the Holy Spirit and God's Word to guide us to all truth, how dare we be less than the most creative, colorful people on earth?

All the components of creativity aren't known, but many of the characteristics are observable. The ability to invent or innovate is part of creativity. A creative person doesn't necessarily invent anything new, although this is possible; but, working with the material available, she or he amplifies it and arrives at a new pattern or new way of looking at known facts. The creative person is able to evaluate critically. He is aesthetically sensitive and flexible. A truly creative person can be happier, freer, because he is bound only by God's restraints and principles.

Creativity training. It begins in your home—a home where you have acknowledged Jesus Christ as your Lord and Savior and have accepted him as Head of your family. In this creative place, you seek to raise children in accordance with his Word, the Bible, and to point them to a personal commitment to Christ and a fuller life with him.

By the time a child begins kindergarten, his attitudes and tastes have been rather well formed. He is becoming selective as his tastes are cultivated. If he has been introduced to the best rather than the mediocre, and shown a wide scope of possibilities rather than having been left alone to pick at random, your child will have an excellent start toward creative adulthood.

Christian parents must train their children to be "all glorious within" (Psa. 45:13); "as plants grown up in their youth . . . as corner stones, polished after the similitude of a palace" (Psa. 144:12).

But something happens to some of our Christian-home children. Their free creative urges are squelched. Their natural curiosity and originality are forced into one pattern after another. Too often they become a name on a church roll, people who remain just names rather than productive persons, because their desire and ability to be unique have died.

Since creativity and its cultivation must be a slow, continuous process, the home is the logical place to start. Here your child feels most at ease. Here he spends most of his time being himself and acting freely.

The direction of your child's development, whether for good or not, will be affected by the types of opportunities that are provided by you.

Children can't independently discover their own potentials or the possibilities of the world of touch, sight, and sound. How is a child to discover that he would like to preach, or that he can visualize the pattern of a great building, or that mathematics will open a world of excitement and challenge? The child may have the capacity, but it is up to you to make sure his discovery of the world and his creative development are not left to chance.

My mother didn't raise a Brahms, Schweitzer, or Rubens. You probably won't either. But God gave my mother's children—and God has given your children—the potential to fill a spot in the world plan that belongs just to them. Whether the spot is filled completely, filled adequately but not splendidly, or not filled at all will be decided in large measure by parents.

You may figure in God's purpose when you train your child to think beyond what has been ingrained by tradition. You, like David, may never build the Temple; but in the child you raise, you may see the fulfillment of God's holiness and glory.

CREATIVITY AND INTELLIGENCE

Although the creative person has been found to be well above the average in intellectual capacity, the exact relationship between creativity and intelligence cannot be shown. If creative ability were assumed from intelligence quota tests, 70 percent of the most gifted youngsters would never be included.

All people are born with an imaginative faculty in varying degrees. The important point for you to remember is not how much creative ability your child has, or even how this supply can be increased, but how you can train your child to put his creative powers to their most productive uses.

To cultivate creativity in a child is not an easy task. I remember the work my mother went to—collecting paints and paper, challenging, designing while-we-work word games. No, she never used the word *creativity,* and in fact I'm not sure she was fully aware of the concept. But God had given her two children and it was fun to channel their activities. It was fun for her to see how much more exciting our colors and words and tinker toy designs were this month than they were the last.

Cultivating creativity requires time and forethought, whether parents choose to experiment in playing word games, molding clay, or writing stories or original songs. Parents must follow with love and understanding the child's attempts to express himself. The child must know that every effort he makes is worth something. In itself the act may have been a mistake, a chance happening. But through each creative self-expression the child will develop initiative, self-control, and imagination.

GUIDING YOUR CHILD

For your child to get the most from the wonders God has placed in him and his world, he must be exposed to them properly, at the right age. He must be allowed to touch, try, fail, and achieve. A child is not born with a fully developed personality. The formation of this personality in large measure is the responsibility of the parents.

On some days the effort may not seem worthwhile, but don't give up too easily or too early. The creative future of your child could depend on your perseverance. Most children are highly imaginative in childhood, and yet many lose that sparkle and become rather uncreative adults. Perhaps one of the single most important reasons for the loss is parents' lack of active encouragement for their children's creative efforts.

"Wow! What a mass of colors. Explain your picture to me."

"Would you like to make up a song with me? You touch the notes on the piano that you want to use. Then we'll work together on a beautiful song. It will be great!"

"You're fun to talk with. You have a lot of interesting thoughts."

A child needs to be guided patiently and consistently as he develops his creative spirit. You believe in your child. You know you can nourish the creative spark within her. You can help that new little girl of yours to form her self-concept. She will know her worth and from this positive self-evaluation will come her praise to her God. "I will praise thee; for I am fearfully and wonderfully made: marvellous are thy works . . . (Psa. 139:14).

Stretch your child's powers by giving him an opportunity to express himself in a wide variety of activities. You aren't stuffing him into a preconceived mold of what your son or daughter ought to be. You are helping your child know more about himself and his relationship to those close to him and to the whole world to which he must relate. The creative process that you are aware of, the exposure to so many important, vital experiences, must always be a part of play, of fun, for your child. This is his only childhood.

This is an ideabook, and hopefully you and your children

will find many of these ideas workable and fun. Use this guidebook as a starting place to open up areas in your own family life where you can be more creative parents. Progress beyond my suggestions to offer your children a start toward fuller, more exciting Christian lives.

As you find freedom and originality through Christ, you want your child to experience this same creativity in his Christ-centered home. In your home you will introduce the pliable child to the important world of expression in which he will live. Art, music, words, play, devotions: in every area you will put before your child the means of expansion, of growth. Raise your child to think, love, react to God and his fellowmen in ways that are uniquely his own. As he reaches his creative potential as a growing child, so will you reach yours as growing parents.

CREATIVITY PRINCIPLES

Each area in which your child's creative curiosity is stirred holds its own excitement and peculiarities. But as you begin thinking about the great avenues open to you and your child, there are some basic principles you can follow, principles applicable to creativity training, no matter what the medium.

1. Present every aspect of your child's life to his Heavenly Father's care. Be sensitive in all your planning so that as parents you will never cease to ask God to guide you in working out his best for your child.

2. Present every possible opportunity to your child, but don't expect him to become a patterned copy of your hopes and dreams. He is an individual and must be accepted as himself for what he can do.

3. Value your child's creative thinking even though it might not seem original from your adult perspective. Work with your child to expand his ideas and correct faulty ones.

4. Provide a home that lends itself to creative activity. Allow the child to be part of his environment by arranging the furniture with him in mind or choosing colors to which he can respond positively.

5. Make your child aware of her worth. She is a child of God and therefore has untold possibilities. Her worth is not measured by her faulty perspective and her halting reading, but by the world of possibilities open to her.

6. Let your child move at his own speed; don't push him toward achievement when he is not ready and couldn't care less.

7. Leave your child time in the day when things aren't planned for her, time when she can think up her own play, work out her own projects, and develop her individuality so that in maturity she will be independent and resourceful.

8. Provide time and space and materials for creative activities. The child should have his own space, his own table, and exciting new textures to explore.

9. Teach her to respect beauty whether it be in a musical composition, an artist's creation, or her completed skyscraper built from her erector set in the middle of the living room floor.

10. Teach her to evaluate her own work. A child should not feel that everything she does is wonderful—nor should she degrade her own efforts. Parents must achieve careful balance so that their criticism does not squelch children's efforts. Nor should they overpraise. Rather, with their gentle suggestions, they should train the child to set a higher achievement goal for her next attempt.

11. Make it necessary for your child to think creatively. If all his thinking is done for him, he will have little incentive to branch out on his own.

12. Realize your child will be an imitator. If you have a fresh outlook on life and are willing to experiment, if you can express yourself and relate to others, if you are the fullest person you can be, your child will have a far greater start toward creative adulthood than all the textbooks, methods, and creative toys dumped on him could ever have.

1

WELCOME TO OUR CREATIVE HOME— SOME IDEAS ON SETTING THE CLIMATE

NORMA'S parents were missionaries who planned to return to their mountain station in less than six months when her mother signed up for a course in home decorating.

"I've always wanted to do something like this," the woman said. "It certainly isn't the most practical thing I could have done with that twenty dollars, and in our primitive situation I won't be able to put much of what I'm learning into practice. But the course is just for me, and I'm enjoying it so much."

Norma watched her mother hunting through magazines for room arrangement ideas for that evening's class. After a few minutes the five-year-old said, "Isn't my mommie pretty when she's happy like that?"

Norma was watching her mother grow as a person. And because Norma has seen that process modeled, she will probably not be afraid to branch out into unfamiliar areas as she grows older. Norma was seeing her mother as a person, not limited to her important role as mother. Norma was getting a wonderfully creative perspective on what it could mean to be a woman.

David was invited by a successful businessman in his congregation to attend a luncheon meeting. In order to help everyone get acquainted, the master of ceremonies suggested they quickly go around the table and tell what their most successful achievement in the last five years had been.

"I made my first million," one man said.

"I opened a branch store."

"I'm first vice president."

David shared his reactions. "I knew eventually it would be my turn and I tried desperately to think of something that would impress these successful people. I'm a pastor, and I knew my small successes in my church would mean nothing to these men. My turn came and I told the truth. 'My most successful achievement has been my marriage and the fathering of my children.' There was dead silence for a long moment before the next man continued with worldshaking achievements. Not one of those men said a word about my success and I've often wondered what they thought.

"But it's true. I've put a lot of work into the two most precious gifts God gave me. I'll never be sorry for those choices."

Are you pleased with the person you are becoming? How inconsistent it would be to try to expand your child's world beyond the boundaries you have set for yourself. Parents who feel they have finished growing will not be the testimony of vitality and awareness they must be. Don't let your child find in his parents a stagnation, a stay-comfortably-seated philosophy of life.

For you, the mother, this continual growth will keep you aware of your world. You won't lose your identity and become only your child's mother or your husband's wife. You will be a whole person, an individual who brings to your marriage and family the wonders of your special personality.

For you, the father, this continual growth will keep you as aware of your home world and the need to succeed there as it will of your career growth. You will not be satisfied to have a successful identity in the church without striving for just as successful an identity as father and as husband.

A creative Christian home is not a gift; it's an achievement—a world created by parents who are willing to exert that extra effort necessary to make a successful family life.

Yes! Most parents want their children to be creative.

Yes! Most also realize that a very important place to start is with the climate, the attitude of their Christ-filled home.

But what goes into making this atmosphere, the attitude, in the home? It certainly isn't the elaborate planning of the home's structure or the furniture that is placed in it. It's not polished manners learned by children or dust-free play areas. It's more than the feelings behind the words, "I love you, son," that daddy says each night as he tucks his little fellow beneath the sheets.

The climate is the composite of words, attitudes, and actions that the child, operating almost entirely in the emotional realm, gathers. She knows when she is more important than the supper dishes when they wait and mother plays with her in a huge cardboard box. She knows when daddy sits and talks to her of the excitement of flying as she paints her crude airplane. A child reaches below the veneer of the home and feels the values and commitments of her parents as they live before her.

The child will estimate his personal worth in light of the pattern his parents set for him. If you evaluate yourself as a second-rate individual, your child's attitude may reflect this. However, if your child senses that you, his parents, are happy people who have assessed your own personal worth and have come to terms optimistically with your potentials and are willing to work to perfect those assets you have discovered, your child too will adopt these attitudes.

As the child grows he will see that everyone within his family is important individually and to the group. He will be learning that he is not the center of the family around which all other people revolve. No, in a creative family each member has a special identity, and has unique contributions to make to the whole group.

MY VERY OWN SPACE

Each child should have a room or a place in the house that is exclusively his, a place he can call his own. In this room with the fuzzy bunny on the door lives a child, an interesting, unpatterned little person who will spend a very few years getting used to his world before he is actually thrown into it. This room can be part of his preparation for adult life.

Your young child's room is, no doubt, an expression of your love for him.

A young mother looked over the freshly painted dresser she had finished for her baby's room and said, "I guess it's silly to go to all this work when she's just newborn, but I just wanted to tell her how much she was loved."

How very important is this first introduction to love, to that extra touch just because you cared. No matter how correct are the temperature of the room, the toys, the lighting, and the furniture to the physical well-being of your son or daughter, without your beautiful extra touches, the most important ingredient in your young child's room is missing.

It's never too early to think about your child's creative

development. A child from his earliest moments is affected by the psychological rather than the tangible world around him. Baby's world is sound and feeling, colors and forms. As he becomes aware of his senses, he can be conditioned and trained.

Here are some ideas to get you started, suggestions that might help expand your child's creativity as his life begins to take shape.

Surround him from the start with exciting, colorful toys that make him want to explore his environment, to reach out and touch, and eventually to ask questions.

Allow her hours of playing, cooing, eye exploration. She can get along quite happily without adults guiding her play.

Even before he responds to anything more than a tone of voice, begin to read him stories. From a voice filled with expression, he will get a foretaste of the adventure in the world of words just ahead of him.

As he learns to talk and tries to imitate the sounds he hears, instead of talking to him in coos and baby talk, give him a chance to hear his language spoken correctly.

As the baby grows, and as the child expands, so should his room or space. Stand back and look at your child's room. Does it reflect his personality? Was he taken into consideration when it was planned? The room should be bright and cheery with enough floor space to allow him to take a pretend trip to Africa or just romp and roughhouse when he wants to. On his walls should be interesting pictures. Some, those of finer art, are permanent pictures, while others change with the seasons or with his interests.

The preschool child needs lots of wandering space and very little furniture. A colorful rug that blends with the room makes playing on the floor more fun. Everything in his area is his size. His feet touch the floor when he sits in his chair or plays at his table. The pictures are at his eye level, not daddy's. He is able to get into his toy box without calling for assistance. There is a place for everything—books, blocks, dolls—but things aren't in their place all the time. This is his room. What he does in it is his own business as long as he follows the cleanup and other simple rules. Of course there will be some breakage and unhappiness in your child's room. That's part of his growth. But this is his world, an often happy and always secure place.

THESE PEOPLE IN MY WORLD

The way a person conducts himself in the company of others, making them feel important and accepted, and how he understands the society of which he is a part, will in some respects help determine his success. No, good manners are not essential to creativity. As a matter of fact, good manners are sometimes equated with regimentation, quite the opposite of creativity. But Christians must be more than creative. The Christian may be able to paint a picture that will reflect something of God's majesty or write free verse on the love of God as he has experienced it. But until he has interacted with people, felt with others, understood others, and communicated with them about his wonderful God, he will have failed to be truly creative. There is nothing that demands more creativity and insight in life than the ability to relate to others.

For a child, encounters with others are elementary. Simple sharing of a jump rope now may set the pattern for sharing the Word of God with a friend later. A harmonious game of cowboys, complete with joyful shouts and broomstick horses, may be the basis of a working group situation later in life. The Bible tells us that even a child makes it known by his doings whether his work will be pure, and whether it will be right (Prov. 20:11). What a child learns as he watches his parents interacting with each other and among their friends, and as he participates in family interactions, will form the basis for his later participation among his peers.

Teach your children to have respect for each person they meet—even those with whom they have little in common. Good manners will be born. These manners, this attitude toward people, is picked up from you in the home before prejudices and preconceptions have had a chance to be planted. You teach by example the appreciation of every person. What a creative difference between the world's view of people and the Christian's.

THE FUN IN MY HOME

The family that is simply a unit of familiar faces watched over, supported, loved—simply the highest duty with which parents have been entrusted—is still lacking something.

Fun!

Fun—what an important element it is. It can make the difference between just raising a family and actually *being* one. And family fun isn't just loving your children, although that's a big part of it. It's more. While love may often come automatically or even from a sense of ought, fun has to be worked at.

Your child may forget her doll house that took most of your Christmas bonus to buy; or he may simply be grateful for the braces that straightened his smile. But when they are grown and look back on the "stuff" that welded mother, father, and children into a family, it will usually be the little things, things that took time together, that they will remember.

Joe sat at the window and watched the rain pound. With his finger he traced the path of drops over the glass. His father looked up from his desk and smiled at his son's concentration and was about to pick up his pen again when the thought struck him, "I've never seen Joey doing that before. Maybe he'll never be so interested in raindrops again." Then for a full ten minutes father and son sat together and made map-paths following the drops' flow. A super highway was over to the left; that windy path through the center must be a race track, and over there . . .

Rarely is there time for family fun. If there were, maybe it wouldn't seem quite so wonderful when the family made time for it. For the Schmid family, it meant setting aside a weekend evening for a family night with their two daughters and infant son.

"We used to have friends in and send the children to

bed. But we realized this was wrong and now we know our most important time is the hours we save for the children," Mr. Schmid said. "We don't talk about business or troubles at meals. Instead we play word games. And we hear the latest jokes from school."

On family night, the five will often have pajama parties. They pop corn or work together on school and community projects. If they're playing games, they often do it by candlelight "just because we like it."

Mr. Schmid summarized, "Love is the thing that makes our family a family. We've found a love that will keep us close no matter what. The true meaning of my home is family. It's what I work for and I guess it's what life is all about."

Take a little time to outline the possibilities for working and playing with your family—for fun. This might call for a lot of rearranging and a little inconvenience, but family fun will fit in. And twenty years from now the memory of family time spent together will still seem important.

1. Analyze just what you did for family fun in the past week. Write it down.
   - Are you pleased with the amount of time spent in family fun?
   - Did all members of the family enjoy most of the family time or was everything enjoyed primarily by the adults? By the children? By one child?
   - Are you pleased with the variety expressed in your family fun times?
   - Are your family fun times creative?

2. Consider each member of your family. Based on his age level and interests, list what each child and adult would do for fun. Ask each member what he or she would do. Compare lists.

3. List the family recreational areas in your community. Don't forget state parks. They make ideal areas for family weekend camping.

4. Think over your family fun equipment. Based on your two lists, should you invest a little money in good equipment and games? It is possible to have a lot of fun

together without spending any money at all, but games that develop skills and group participation and competition will never be a mistake. When you are evaluating your resources, look within your own four walls. Try hide and seek, a treasure hunt, a newspaper-costume party: simple fun activities that can be age-graded so that most children and adults enjoy them.

5. Make some definite plans. Set aside the time. Know what you want to do in that time slot. Don't allow anything to get in the way of your planned fun time together. Joe, vice president of a large company, was often asked to speak. "I'd look at the date the group was asking for and there would be nothing on the calendar, so I would accept. Those free days were the days I would have spent with my family," Joe said. "Finally I realized what was happening. I began to write family days on the calendar. Now when I get calls, if the dates conflict with those family dates, I simply say, 'I'm sorry, but I've got an important previous commitment.' "

Always remember that God's basic unit in society is the family. Through this unit you have the opportunity to raise your children to think as mature, well-rounded Christians. Your home in your community may be the only example of Christianity your neighbors see.

A good family may become an excellent missionary outreach unit—your home, the only real expression on your block of what God can mean today. Your home—the living expression to your children of what God can mean in their lives, a model for the days when they will be structuring their own family units.

COULD THIS WORK IN YOUR FAMILY?

There's a whole world of things a family can do together. With a little imagination and research, lists are easy to make. The difficult part comes in carrying out well-laid plans. Parents must give their child a well-rounded diet of experiences, a range of activities that will stretch him into knowing more about himself and about the people around him—indeed about the big world in which he lives.

As children and adults plan family activities together, the adults should make sure that all the planning isn't done exclusively with the children in mind. After all, this is mother's and father's family, and they ought to be not just planners but participants as well.

A little effort, some creative thinking, a revised schedule, and maybe some of these suggestions will help you discover the wonders of growing and working together as a family. Don't stop with this list, because the possibilities are as wide and varied as your imagination. Be creative—expand!

1. Give each child a garden, a space where he can grow his favorite flowers or vegetables. This area can be a part of the lawn, a flower box, even just a wide-mouthed jar. As the child tends his plants, he'll be learning. Related activities will have to be introduced to hold your preschooler's fleeting interest. He could draw pictures of what he hopes will grow. Mother and he could make a garden book filled with all the things they would grow if they had space.

What a wonderful firsthand way to teach a child about God's creation, his care for plants and animals, and his care for children.

A young elementary student might enjoy studying about the worms and bugs that are able to live in the type of soil found in his garden.

And don't forget a Saturday field trip to a farm.

Not everything a garden can teach a child can be predicted by the parent. My father gave my brother and me our small plots in his larger garden on a day when I was just furious at Jim, my brother. I decided to use my plot to pay him back for whatever awful thing he had done to me by planting spinach—a lot of spinach. He couldn't eat the stuff without gagging, but my mother would never allow us to waste any food. So I knew that if my spinach grew, he would have to eat it. So what did I learn? First, that spinach takes two seasons to grow to maturity, and second, that I couldn't possibly stay mad at my brother that long.

2. Daily cleanups can be part of family growth. Sure, it's easier if you do it yourself, but your child needs to know that this is her home and she must contribute to it.

Although work is work—and we're just fooling ourselves if we think we can convince children that making beds, dusting, and sweeping are fun—we can add a little interest to it. Ramona's mother used to hide a little blue bird before cleaning started. Then, when the bird was found in the process of cleaning, mother and daughter would stop for a snack. The work got done, but there was a bit of fun too.

My mother and I would play word games while we worked. She would say a word and I would have to come up with another word that began with the same letter with which her word had ended. Or for even more fun—we would sing our conversations! Sometimes as I got older we would sing in rhyming couplet. Again, it was a way to bind us together as parent and child and get the work done at the same time.

3. Family camping has become a national vacation option. Local chapters of camping organizations such as the Campers and Hikers Association sponsor camping all year round for the outdoor-loving family. What an excellent way to get to know families who are not within our Christian subculture. But remember, if a witness is to be made, your family must have something special to offer.

Many churches are sponsoring camping as a family retreat idea. They combine family recreation and Christian fellowship. The child gets every benefit of a weekend at camp, but you have the opportunity to be his counselor, to show him the wonders of God's living, growing outdoors.

If you take your family camping, make it a different experience. Remember, checkers can be played at home. Instead, why not take a night flashlight hike, or have a scavenger hunt, or a nature study? A telescope and a child's book of constellations can open a whole new world to a youngster.

Jerry used to make up his own stories about the constellations and share them with his family. As he went through the elementary grades, his parents encouraged him to record the best ones. They helped him expand the nights under the stars into a creative writing activity.

4. Mealtime is the only time many families talk. But why not try a switch? Have a "monastic" meeting at which no

one is allowed to talk. Let the family members try to anticipate each other's needs and see just how sensitive they can be. In this type of quiet, often more is learned by young family members than in the fun and clamor of regular meals. Don't try this without explaining the whole reason behind it. (Preschool children are not old enough to enjoy or benefit from this suggestion.)

5. Work on a family service project. Lancaster County has a "Fresh Air" program every summer. Children of all races are brought from the high-rise areas of Philadelphia and New York City and placed in good small town or rural homes. The child stays for a week or two, and in many cases returns to the same family year after year. Children in both situations—visitors or hosts—learn to get along together and to share with children of different cultures. They learn firsthand that not everyone is as privileged as they.

Recently two inner-city Spanish girls spent two weeks of their high school training living in a large suburban home surrounded by trees and farmland. Each day they would work with me and other people involved in writing and editing Sunday curriculum. The idea was for them to learn of the options education allowed. And they learned! Norma, a beautiful sixteen-year-old, told me that no woman in her family had ever worked outside the block. She wanted to be a lawyer—she felt she had the ability and her Spanish people had need for her services. But before the two weeks with us, in which she saw many women using gifts that God had given them, she hadn't thought her dream was possible. She returned home to continue working toward a goal she knew could be reached.

But the surprise was what we learned from them. Those of us who are especially interested in teenagers pumped the girls about their interests, fears, ideas, goals, attitudes, prejudices. We learned about community respect and respect for families as it is defined in their Spanish culture. We learned what they wanted from the church.

A service project often works both ways. Don't allow your children to feel they are totally the givers and others the receivers. Help them by your own modeling to see how much all of us can learn from each other. As Norma left the beautiful home in which she was staying, she said, "I'll miss you guys, but I sleep better at home. It's too quiet around here—no one in the streets, nothing happening. The city's a great place to live."

There are so many potential projects for families. I knew one family that gathered toys for poor children for special holidays. The family painted and fixed the usable toys. Even the preschooler washed the dirty toys and held wheels that had been glued into place.

Don't overlook the projects suggested by your newspapers. One second-grade girl gathered clothes from neighbors for Greek families during one severe winter. She and her mother sewed buttons and seams to get the clothes into the best possible condition before they were sent. "This project originated with Dolores," the child's mother said. "She heard a missionary speak, came home for her wagon, and started out to the neighbors. My first response was 'Isn't that cute!' But then I realized what a great opportunity it was to share in her missionary zeal. Our family sent about 2000 pounds of blankets to Greece that year. I've learned never to underestimate the impact of the right project for the right child."

6. Would a "stitch and chatter" club work in your church or community? The object is to build communication between mothers and daughters from age eight or nine through junior high and high school. At the club each mother could teach a skill of her own, for example, knitting, candlemaking, tole painting. Each girl would learn from whichever mother was teaching something that interested her. Mothers will discover the keen minds of their children and appreciate some of their growing-toward-maturity qualities. Girls will learn the wisdom, skills, and patience of their parents.

The women in my community had a stitch and chatter club for the women when I was growing up. I was the only girl in the area, so when I was about ten, my mother started including me in the group of women. They would bring their mending and knitting. And I learned! From Ruth I learned to use transparent oils to color photographs. From

Eleanor I learned how to tell a funny story. But I never learned how to darn socks—everyone was just too busy talking.

7. How about a walk through your backyard or a local park? What a creative experience this can be for a small child guided by an observant adult. Show the child the insects' eggs clumped on the underside of a leaf. Teach him to make a whistle from a long grass and how to preserve a colored leaf.

With each of these outdoor adventures, the child learns more about God. He becomes saturated with nature's wonder. When he matures, he may paint the beauty of a tree or set a waterfall to music, but he may never appreciate their wonder more than he does right now.

8. How about a pet when the child is old enough to take care of it? Read to her and have her read books on how to take care of the particular pet. Be creative. List the ways a goldfish in a crowded apartment could add to your child's education.

9. Especially in our Christian environment, parents often get the opportunity to entertain exciting and unique people. A missionary who isn't monopolized by the adults can become a hero in your son's eyes. When you entertain a visiting musical group your children might take an added interest in their music lessons. In many ways visitors broaden your child's world. When he sees his parents at ease with visitors, he will learn to mature into the same type of relaxed, natural host.

I grew up thinking that half the missionaries in the world had at one time or another slept in my bed. I fit perfectly on the couch. I didn't mind losing my bed a bit—the couch was downstairs so I got to stay up later!

We had some funny experiences. One man walked right through the living room with only a towel wrapped around him and announced to all gathered there that he was going to take a "little rinse."

In the days before garbage pickup, my mother used to cut hers into little pieces and my father would bury it at the base of the garden. One missionary left to tell people in other homes that he had never in his life seen such a housekeeper. "Mrs. LeFever is so neat," his words came back to us, "that she even dices her garbage."

So when your church needs a place to sleep a visiting pastor, missionary, drama group—volunteer. These people can expand your concept of family and the thinking of your children.

10. Take advantage of the miles around your home. Many school teachers would be happy to give you names of places that children have studied within a 100-mile radius. Field trips aren't soon forgotten. Automobile clubs will help you plan a family tour of your state. Many towns have brochures that include activities of special interest to children.

I'm from Lancaster, Pennsylvania. It was the capital of the United States for one day. People say it has the richest farmland in the United States. It's geographically between Gettysburg and Valley Forge. In the county live the oldest and wealthiest group of Amish people in the states. I met a lot of people when I worked at the *Lancaster New Era* as a reporter, and I never ceased to be amazed when people would tell me, "We've lived here a year, and we haven't gotten around to seeing the Amish yet." Or, "My kids wouldn't be interested in history." Or, "I try to avoid the historic areas at all costs. Too many tourists."

That makes me sad. It also makes me a bit mad! How many opportunities for our children are sitting almost outside our doors, and we don't make use of them?

11. Keep a rainy-day drawer filled with interesting things for children. Spools, cones from the inside of twine rolls, colored paper, and this list goes on. Children often have great ideas for do-it-themselves art projects after they see creative materials. Remember—rainy days only. That keeps the drawer special.

12. There are lots of special-day parties that parents can dream up to make a family week more exciting. How about a thank-you party thrown by the parents for the children in appreciation for their help around the house? A comic-strip party would be fun. Each member must dress and act like his favorite cartoon character for an evening. Use newspapers for guidance on the costumes.

My mother once planned "a year in two weeks" when some missionary children stayed with us for that time. We had New Year's Eve and Valentine's Day and Easter and so on through the two weeks. It was great fun for her own kids, but I doubt those children who spent much of their lives in a small mission compound in a developing nation will ever forget it.

THE CHILD AND PLAY

A complete definition of play as it applies to small children would be difficult to formulate. It is not a time of free, random relaxation. It is the bulk of his existence, and what happens during this period of his training will affect his physical, emotional, social, intellectual, and even spiritual development for the rest of his life.

Make a list of things your children learn from play. You'll be surprised. I'll get you started and you add five more:

- Children learn to do things for themselves—a type of self-mastery that will help them feel good about themselves.
- Children learn to get along with others, living by the rules of the group but also feeling good about themselves as individuals.
- Children learn how to meet and overcome obstacles. Play is preparation for life. If the parent makes everything run smoothly—no win/lose situations—the children will not be prepared for the world of business, parenthood, or Christian service.

What kinds of play do you remember from your early childhood? For me, it was the games when parents were not visible and I was creating my own world. I knew, I suppose, that parents were there somewhere, so I wouldn't get hurt, but they did not impose their wishes and their ideas on my play. I remember playing hospital on the front porch of my Aunt Arro's house. I remember building a hideout under a big pine tree. I remember being a horse, a leader of an outlaw group, a boxer, a city planner and builder.

Play, of course, grows as the child grows. It begins with spontaneous movements and stimulation of the sense organs. As he reaches two, he enters the toy age. At three he prefers solitary play. He is able to participate in parallel play with a few others. And then the fun time! By four he is ready for social or group play. Can adult life be far behind?

Be careful with play. Let your child take the lead. I suspect that some parents can stifle creativity in a child by structuring too much play time and by participating in too much of that time. The child needs time to move at his own speed and do what he wants to do.

Play is not just materials. It is what happens within the child as he expresses himself. It is controlled emotional outlet through which the child introduces himself to the world and finds just where he fits. John wants to be a farmer because he has played farmer and knows it's exciting to play in the warm mud. And when Johnny plays daddy, he will be copying what he sees in his own father. Whether that image is honestly Christian or not makes no difference. John will take this as the correct image of the Christian father. Children learn by acting out what they have been exposed to. For years I wanted to be a truck driver because my Uncle Lloyd worked with trucks and he taught me to make shadow monsters on the wall. To this day, large trucks and the people who drive them are surrounded by a positive aura of romance left over from my play days.

Children's play is endless repetition, but each new expression, each character and play vocabulary enlarges the child's world. For instance, parents can instill a love for Bible stories in their children by encouraging the child to play character parts. Or with older children, ask questions like: "How would you feel as a girl coming to Jesus, like the boys and girls long ago were able to do? Let's think now. What are some of the things you would like to tell him?"

Play, in addition to providing a good emotional outlet, encourages and guides the children's creative imagination. The parent who is aware of this will be able to provide a balance for the child in his purchase of creative toys and in his suggestions for play.

Play gives the child an opportunity to grow in social understanding and cooperation as he matures and interacts with other children. A parent who carefully cultivates in his child the ability to play with others and by himself will lay the foundation for self-reliance as the child matures.

Space in some of our urban areas is a problem. The last generation's ballpark now has a building covering it. The backyard of my first home is now a parking lot for a huge supermarket. But actually, the child doesn't need much space. A small yard, a playroom, a family room in the basement, or half a living room can become a jungle or an Indian reservation for a playing child. Children are creative even without adult intervention. Most children can learn to be creative with a limited amount of play space and very little equipment. I remember when Jim and I both had measles at the same time; we used our sheets to make huge tents over our beds. Our mother was wise enough to see the fun in sheets attached to light fixtures and window shades. For two weeks Jim and I "camped out." Measles were fun—well, sort of.

In addition to creative small-space activity, vigorous activity is needed for growing bodies. With this in mind, many parents find it important to invest in some sturdy play apparatus.

Either way, a child's play areas and his toys should tax his imagination. Many a child has left his battery-powered cars to play in a discarded paper box. The box can be anything and take him anywhere he wants to go. Life is more exciting when it borders on the almost-land. Inside that box, away from the world of grownups, he can think as far as he wants to. Freedom is a child's most priceless possession, and it's one grownups try hardest to take from him.

In the selection of toys that will be given to your child, remember that children are people—people with individual personalities. Your child's toys should correspond to his interests, his skills, and his potential skills. Tempt your children to stretch their imaginations and expand their own exciting ideas.

Some toy suggestions just to get your list started:

dump truck that can be filled with anything
unbreakable doll that can be washed and dressed
bright balls
cartons that are large enough to hide a small child
plastic bottles that can be filled with anything
building blocks or sticks
lettered blocks
old clothes
stilts
wagon
climbing equipment
sandbox
wheel toys

Often swings are not suggested in preferred lists of children's toys because young children require too much help from others to make them usable.

2

THE CREATIVE
WORLDS OF
READING

THROUGH the mishaps of Yertle the Turtle, the wanderings of Toby Tyler, or the antics of Dumbo the flying elephant, a child's imagination pushes into unexplored areas. As he is read to (and later as *he* reads) the world opens before him. During the one life your child will live, there will be open to him a hundred other lives in which he can participate vicariously—the lives and worlds in books.

"I read books to my daughter long before she could speak," a mother said. "Her first words were the predictable mama and dada, but her very next words were the complete sentence, 'I want a book.' She did and she still does."

What happens if our children can't read? Whole areas of their imagination will never be expanded. Television will draw the pictures for them so they will never have to think originally. Their heroes will remain stereotyped and underdeveloped. Most of all, they'll never feel the friendship that can be established between children and their favorite book characters, a real companionship because the children participated in the formation of that character.

"*The Lion, the Witch, and the Wardrobe* by C. S. Lewis used to be my favorite book," said Phillip, now a senior high student. "I read it first in fourth grade and I've been through it twice since. I had beautiful pictures in my head. The world Lewis painted really existed for me. Then it was on TV. All my pictures were ruined by someone else's cartooned version of the story. My mind pictures were better, and now they are ruined."

When reading is so wonderful to some children, why do others find it so difficult—so boring? Sometimes parents must accept partial responsibility. A child's reading ability will correspond to his thinking and talking ability. The parent who makes an effort to talk to his child in story and in complete conversations will actually be teaching his child prereading skills.

Much of the talking will be done by the parent in the beginning, but more and more, the child will participate. As he talks, his understanding expands. Two cows in a picture become a cow and a baby cow. Then, finally the baby cow becomes a calf. Most children who enjoy reading have come from homes where they were encouraged to handle books. They were read to, talked over what they read, and took active part in family conversation.

Sure, reading is important, but why include a whole chapter on reading in a creativity book. How creative is reading since it's the book's author who does the work? Nothing new, or at least visually new, is created by the child. Right?

Not really. Think what happens when a child reads or is read to. He draws mental pictures and often paints them with originality. He meets and forms friendships with book-children his own age, within and foreign to his culture. He will often expand a story he likes into a day-fantasy in which he writes the sequel and actually becomes the hero. I remember when I owned Black Beauty and almost singlehanded, saved my horse from destruction!

Words tempt children to go farther and farther outside what used to be themselves—into so many new areas. Without books, these worlds would never be open to them.

In training your child to read widely, in putting before him the temptation of a good story, you are aiding his creative development as greatly as you ever will through any medium.

As Christian parents, you not only want your child to be a reader, but you also want him to be reading the right things. First books are important. The books that mother reads to him about the love of God and God's care for him might well form a basic theology for the child.

Little children understand far beyond their speaking vocabularies before they develop any reading skills. The importance of good books and reading in the young child's life cannot be overemphasized. Good books help you teach ideas that will influence the child for life. The Bible says that as a person thinks in his heart, so is he (Prov. 23:7). "Whatsoever things are honest, whatsoever things are just, whatsoever things are pure, whatsoever things are lovely, whatsoever things are of good report; if there be any virtue, if there be any praise, think on these things" (Phil. 4:8).

Since the child often patterns his reading habits after his

parents, take a good look at your library. Does it serve the values you hold supreme? As your child becomes more observant, what is he going to see reflected in his father's reading? Just as truly as books begin to mold the child, so do they continue to influence him as he grows into adolescence and adulthood. Francis Bacon declared, "Reading maketh a full man." Through reading the imagination is fed and the outgrowth of imagination—creativity—is nurtured. If their early literature is vivid, genuine, and presented with variety, children will look excitedly for additional areas in which to exercise newfound skills. A love of reading will have been born.

In a very real sense, children will mature with their books. Through the book heroes and other characters, they will obtain new insights into the world and into themselves. As boys and girls live through crises in the stories they read, they discover a new maturity within themselves that yearns to be part of the world of deeds.

A child's reading should live—it's something special. A home with young children should be saturated with reading material, filled with exciting pictures that tempt the child to discover the words that explain them. When he hears what those words mean, when he realizes that it will someday be possible for him to understand the meaning, all this helps mold a child.

"We got Davie a number of expensive Christmas presents," his mother said. "The one that has been most lasting was his own monthly subscription to a children's magazine. He is still amazed by the whole process of mail delivery and the fact that every month the mailman finds him. Because the magazines are his, he saves them when he has finished reading them. They are about the only things that are neatly stacked in his glorious mess of a room."

Davie's parents have used the articles in his magazine to spark family trips. After a story about buried treasure, the family went to a museum and looked at some real treasures. An article about Japan led to a visit to the home of a Japanese woman who lived in their town and attended their church.

Perhaps as Davie enters third grade and spends more time on history and geography, he will use his stack of magazines for research and picture projects.

We didn't get many magazines in our home, but every month the *National Geographic* arrived. My brother and I knew the rules. We were free to cut anything out of any magazine for a school project except the articles on the Holy Land. For decades my father has kept those articles for himself! After we were finished with the current issue it was piled in the basement to await the next report. I remember my progression through the magazine. As a tiny child I enjoyed the pictures. In early elementary school I was able to understand the groupings of pictures—all about birds or all about a country. On to fourth grade and the captions became important. It wasn't until I was almost out of high school that I began to read the whole articles that accompanied the pictures. That magazine, a few important teachers, several books, and my mother formed the unique team that got me excited about words.

CHOOSING THE CHILD'S BOOKS

You can influence the reading habits of your child in many ways. First, make the climate of your home conducive to reading. A simple thing like a crawl-up-and-cuddle-into chair near a colorful selection of books can do the trick.

Can you take time to read to your child every day from his book choice? Children often respond to stories and books that match their interests rather than yours. Julie was in fourth grade when she asked her mother to read *The Robe* to her. "There were parts that she didn't understand," her mother said. "But she loved the story. I would read right up to an exciting spot and make her go to bed. It was a great trick but it backfired. She got me so into the book that I couldn't sleep until I found out what happened. So I would read for hours, and then go back and recap for her the next night."

Children are not always capable of listing the reasons for liking or not liking a book, but they can't be tricked into liking a book when they know it doesn't please them.

Remember that if your child doesn't enjoy the book, no matter how high an opinion you have of it or how classic its adult appeal, it is not the right book. If a child puts it down, bored with its content, anxious to go on to something more interesting, something he understands better, the book has failed the supreme test.

First books gain their appeal through their sound, as in alliteration, or in the giggly tones of the nonsense words of Dr. Seuss. The rhythm of language intrigues children. The more they hear the story, the better the sounds become.

It there is touch appeal, such as a fuzzy duck for them to actually run their hands over, so much the better.

As parents introduce their children to the Bible stories that are applicable to their child's age, they should keep in mind the characteristics of their child. For instance, the preschooler should hear the *clippity-clop* of Jesus' donkey as he rides into the city. Or as she hears the story of the baby Jesus wrapped warm and cuddly, she might listen to the new baby breathe. Softly, softly. *Shhhhhh*: don't wake the sleeping baby.

By the time a child reaches the first grade, his books can have from 150 to 200 different words. As you choose your child's books, make sure his first, easy books are more than easy. The content should appeal to your child—who also watches Saturday morning television. The language should be picture-making and rhythmical. Each book should say, "Don't stop with me. Try something else. Read another story, and grow."

READING PRINCIPLES

These principles will help you interest your child in words, stories, and finally reading.

1. Know your child's interests. Recognize him as an individual personality and choose his books accordingly. Jim was never much of a reader. Give him a choice between a truck and a book, and the truck would win every time. I suppose that's still true today. But from about fifth grade on, he read *Popular Mechanics*. That magazine is aimed at adult readers, but because he cared about the subject, he could master it. I wonder if he had had books about building, cars, or speed as a very young child, if the whole world of reading would now be more exciting to him.

2. Allow your child time to read, but never push him. Reading should always be fun, never a drudgery. Be sure he has a place to read where he can be comfortable and uninterrupted.

3. Recently a new baby was born to Rose and Gary. They had two children, ages five and seven. What wonderful books were available to them to prepare their youngsters for the newcomer: books about how babies are born. Books carefully explaining how brothers and sisters can help care for the baby. Books on the feelings some children have when a new family member arrives.

Choose some of your books with special events and special problems in mind. If she is having trouble getting along with others, perhaps a book about a girl with similar problems will help her. If divorce is touching her life, provide books that would help her deal with this problem.

4. Give your child a wide variety from which to choose. Never tell him what to read. Just make books available and allow him to do the picking.

5. Never compare children's reading habits. While young Marianne may find nothing so exciting as a book on dolls in other lands, her brother may be interested primarily in outdoor life.

In one family the third-grade son thought Chevy cars were about the most interesting things in the world. He made models of them, drew pictures, sat behind the wheel of his father's. But books held little appeal because they weren't about his beloved car. One day he and his father visited the Chevrolet showroom and came home with booklet after booklet filled with information about the car.

He and his mother spent several hours cutting pictures and writing a notebook all of their own about the cars, where they might go, what made them run, and all their specialized vocabulary. Don't be afraid of using technical language with children. It acts as an added incentive to reading; they love it.

After her daughter had seen the play *Medea,* based on Greek mythology, one mother brought her a child's book on Greek myths to sustain her interest. Not long afterward the mother was taken off guard when she asked her daughter where the sun was at high noon. "Oh, noon is when Phoebus-Apollo is at his highest peak in his ride across the sky," was her answer.

6. Help your child become a discriminating reader. If he has been exposed only to the comic books, he will hardly want to sit down with a book like *Treasure Island*.

As your child grows toward his teen years when such a wide variety of reading material is available to him, when he couldn't possibly read everything in his interest areas, he will know how to choose his books wisely.

7. Don't assume that because your child has learned to read, he no longer needs to be read to. His understanding is way beyond his reading ability. A well-read story that sparkles with interest will hold any child's attention. Now, as an adult, Joan looks back on the times when she would sit and listen to her mother reading aloud to her father from books that were beyond the child's understanding. "I listened anyway because I liked the tone of her voice. I could tell books had something wonderful to say because mother seemed to love them so much. I couldn't wait until I was old enough to understand all the words."

8. Recognize that, as the child's interests grow, so should the depth of the books he is reading. Donald was still in second grade when he asked me, "Which do you like better? The brontosaurus or the tyrannosaurus? I'm a brontosaurus man myself."

9. Know what books, especially in the religious area, are being produced. The market used to be very limited. That's no longer true. Go to your local Christian bookstore and take a critical look at what's happening in children's books. They sparkle. Their message is wedded successfully to the story so that neither can exist without the other. The art is colorful, imaginative. Times are changing. If you overlooked Christian children's books a decade ago, that is no reason why you can't now reconsider them.

10. Allow time after reading for discussion or questions. In this way your child will begin to verbalize what he has learned. As he reads on his own, he may continue sharing with you. It's a great way to keep abreast of what your child is reading and how well he understands.

CHILDREN AND POETRY

A child responds naturally to poetry. Listen to his word pictures now, before the worn-out adjectives and tired clichés we use have cluttered up his speech. If he doesn't have just the right word to express something, he will express his response in words and sounds he does know. That freshness comes close to poetry. No wonder he loves it when his books are written in rhyme. Nothing fascinates a child like the singing quality, the melody, and movement behind it. Good words that place their emphasis on expression and unusual arrangement of syllables delight a child as he tries to repeat the combinations.

When you give your child his first book of poems, whether it's a child's version of the Psalms, Mother Goose rhymes, or nonsense verses, remember that poetry is a literature form that must be read aloud to be appreciated. When you read, make the poems sing. Your child should be able to hear the river and practically feel the wind on his face.

Poetry should be a happy experience. For a child to appreciate it to its fullest, he must hear many good poems and memorize a few of his special ones.

"I wouldn't call it good poetry," said Sylvia. "In fact, I'm not sure that today I would even call it poetry, but I remember in kindergarten, my teacher taught me several poems. They've come with me through the years, and I find myself passing along their obvious wisdom to my own children.

Little Danny Donkey
It's sad enough for tears
'Cause little Danny Donkey
Doesn't like to wash his ears.

"I wonder if I would have remembered great poems as easily if I had been introduced to them in third grade instead of later?"

No wonder a child responds to poetry. The rhythm is his rhythm. The poem's unique expression helps the child reach out beyond to find something foreign and wonderful.

PLAYING THE STORY

"I want to play doctor this time," Jimmy pouted. "I'm the one what built this here hospital and I gotta all the time be sick."

Children play stories all the time. Why not occasionally play with them in acting out books that have been read? Maybe the characters won't do exactly what they did in the story, but that's not important. What is important is what happens to the child when he acts the part of his favorite character. For him, the living room becomes a meadow with a brook flowing through it. He is taking care of his sheep. Now he helps one over the stream. With another who has hurt his leg, he will gently oil the wound and carry it for a little while. As the parent watches or participates—perhaps as a sheep—he will understand that his child is learning more completely from this role-taking than he ever could from just listening to the story.

There are many reasons for encouraging your child to play the story. First, she will enjoy it. It is as successful with one child, as she seeks satisfaction in her individual drama, as it is when all the family's children take part.

Through roleplaying children learn what it feels like to be people other than themselves. The Old Testament comes alive. The child understands better the problems of a Mexican boy who has just entered his class and can speak only Spanish. He feels what it is like to be the father or the mother of a little baby. In roleplay it doesn't make much difference which sex a child plays. Imagination is wide enough to go either direction.

"We were studying the life of Moses," Stanley said. "Our three kids were learning at their own levels. But each of them was having difficulty putting all the little pieces into the story. For example, John was too young to understand how the baby in the basket was the man who led the walk across the dry river. We decided to play the story in a park. Of course, our youngest still had problems with the age span. That's fine. We don't want to force his maturation process—even if that were possible.

"But our two older children gained a real understanding of the flow of Exodus. It came alive to them. Now they are able to place the events in Moses' life in order. They have a greater understanding of his spiritual growth.

"I think we will always think of the oak tree as Egypt!"

What a natural way to teach a child about the stories of the Bible! But just as important as the story content, is the way he can be taught to feel as others feel, and to put into practice the lessons behind the stories he has learned.

THE PICTURE POTENTIAL

The world of pictures becomes a reality to a child at approximately fourteen months. It's easy to introduce him to different kinds of art and many varieties of color combinations.

In his Bible story books, special care must be given to make sure your child is getting the best any publisher has put out. Many of his first books will be chosen for their looks rather than for what they say. And the "look" part of his life will not be expanded if you limit what you buy to a single or narrow group of publishers.

The avant garde in children's religious publications might not always be produced by a publishing company that adheres strictly to your theological persuasions. Often this doesn't matter in children's reading because the theology doesn't come through. Of course, you will want to be concerned enough about your child's reading to carefully check materials you'll be giving him. Spend a few hours in a number of bookstores. See what's available and what your child will learn from the pictures and the words of his early books.

My husband bought a set of first books and records for a child's birthday gift. The materials were thoroughly evangelical, but the parents told him they would rather have him return the gift and buy books that were totally literal in their artistic presentation. "We want our son to see the stories as close to the way the people and places looked, as possible," they said. "We're afraid the whimsical quality of the art will make Jerry put the Bible stories into the same category as books about the Easter bunny and Santa Claus."

Jack totally disagreed with their reasoning, but he was impressed with the thought they had given to what they wanted their son to see in his books. They were not leaving his exposure totally to chance.

Choose picture books for their storytelling qualities, the familiar subject matter, and the elementary coloring. Be aware of the advancement in reproduction techniques that are calculated to appeal to the child—pictures that the child understands and yet that allow room for him to fill in with his own imagination. Ask whether a given type of art would stretch or limit your child.

Children like having the pictures that represent what they are reading right next to the text. With details, they are literalists. If there were three bears in the story, there had better be three bears in the picture.

As children are exposed to good art of many varieties, they will respond to them and their tastes will expand.

Physical aspects of the book are important. It shouldn't be so big that the child can't handle it easily. It should be sturdily made. If a book becomes a friend, it will be used a lot. Make sure it will hold up under sticky hands and many falls. White space around the illustrations and throughout the book will give the story an uncluttered look—the book seems clean, inviting, to a child as he approaches it. Big type helps the beginning reader to read more easily without assistance.

If a child is to come with proper respect to his books, he must know how to take care of them himself. He should have a bookshelf within his reach that is exclusively for his books. From his parents' example, he will learn care and treatment.

When he gets a new book you will teach him to open it properly so the back won't be broken. My father published our family genealogy in a hardcover edition. The first edition came out when I was a youngster. I remember sitting at the table and following his directions as we opened each of the thousand books that would be sent across the United States and Canada. "You can't depend on people knowing how to do this," my father said. "We'll do it for them and make sure the book lasts as long as possible." It was fun knowing something that, according to my father, some grownups didn't know.

If the child helps mend the torn pages, he will understand how precious a possession his book is.

A high school freshman packed away all her junior high books. "I'm going to keep them in the attic for awhile," she said. "Eventually I'll give them to other girls who will read them. But they are my friends, and right now it would be like giving a child up for adoption if I gave them away."

THE LIBRARY

Children's books are expensive, much too expensive to allow some families to buy as many as they would like or even as many as their children could use. The library is the answer. More and more town libraries are catering to the young reader. There are picture books to interest the beginning reader. Reading rooms with little chairs and tables for the pint-sized looker are often supplied. He can go and sit in the wide, spacious room and be surrounded by books specially displayed for his pleasure. In many libraries there is a place where toys, a play room, and books form an exciting trio to tempt your child to read.

One city has a Tuesday coffee hour for parents while their tots listen to a trained storyteller read from a variety of books. The enthusiasm of the children shows. In this type of situation it would be impossible for the hundred children to see the pictures, but through the living visual aid of the reader who puts her all into every story, none is needed.

A California church pushes its church library the same way. Every Sunday night before the evening service people gather to hear church library books read. There is no discussion, only the stories. The readers are excellent and very young people to grandparents sit enthralled listening to a story their minds make live.

Some libraries offer special courses for children, such as a finger painting session once a month where the child paints as he hears a story read. Usually these graded sessions are held on Saturday.

Does your child have his own library card? It's a good idea.

He feels pride of ownership—it's all his and with it he can borrow any book he pleases from his library.

It's too bad that most church libraries do not have as much creative thought put into them as public libraries. Christian books aren't dull, but would you know that if you were a child let loose in your church library?

Begin by looking at the books. Does it look like an antique collection? Concerned parents could help build up the contemporary collection of children's books by pledging a book a month for a year to the library.

Could you paint the library, decorate the walls with colorful book jackets, advertise books in the church bulletin?

If the room can't be updated, could you get a colorful book-mobile to wheel from room to room on Sundays? A child should know from the first that there are excellent Christian books that are as much fun to read as those he will find in the secular world.

3
PAINT ME
A PICTURE

"CHRISTMAS just wasn't Christmas," my husband Jack said, "unless I got art materials of some sort. Crayons, large tablet of paper, paints, origami paper—it didn't matter what the art materials looked like as long as they were there."

Lucky man. His parents realized how important it was to their son to express himself with colors and textures, and they did all they could to feed that hunger in him. "I loved *Reader's Digest* covers," Jack said. "For years I collected them because they represented a type of fine art that I didn't find in most Christian magazines. They were for me a wondrous gallery. They said, 'Keep looking. There is more in color, shape, and form than you now know. Have fun while you're looking!' "

Christians should be among the most artistic, creative people in the world. But not many of us are. We have too few Christian writers, painters, musicians.

Once in awhile a Christian contribution gleams like a morning star. But far too often the little that we produce could more honestly be compared to a firecracker than a star. Why? Could it have something to do with many of our basic attitudes toward the arts?

Parents should know about the aesthetic areas into which their child can delve, but before they can aid the child in this exploration, they must have clearly stated for themselves their response to artistic expression.

Does God call a person to be a painter, a photographer, an actor? Yes. And when we encourage our children to develop talents and gifts in these areas, we also know that we must back them with tremendous amounts of prayer. The artist may see things more vividly, or with more intensity, than the rest of us. He or she will face the temptations unique to areas in which the self plays such an important creative role.

The divine Artist created a world in which no two things are exactly alike: our personalities, a dandelion, a snowflake—all are expressions of God's creation. Surely now, as his followers, we have the right, in fact the duty, to be well trained so that the world may see a bit of what God can do in a life given to his color-and-form control.

Perhaps the fear of aesthetics is not altogether ill

founded. We create something and it reflects us, not the Creator. How easy it is for us to begin worshiping the God behind the image we see created, and end up worshiping the image.

Yes, there are dangers in any form of creativity. But because of those dangers, do we give up a whole area of our great heritage? For some, the answer has been yes. For many, many more, the answer is no. The Christian in art should always use his work to point to God rather than down to the ugly changing world that many have made their kingdom. Art viewers must learn to discriminate between pop-art, a craving for total abandonment in the name of freedom, and truly great art. The latter is reflected in the works of people who have poured from their depths, willing for the cause of creativity to bear their deepest feelings, aspirations, loves within the disciplines of that art.

Art isn't something we can take or leave. We're surrounded with evidences of art in nature, in our sacraments, in the massive buildings in which we worship and study. Art belongs to us. We Christians cannot divorce ourselves from the world of people. We are endowed with the ability to react to art, as are those who do not know our God. But in a deeper sense, to a Christian who appreciates the arts, "the artistic experience may become . . . a more thrilling experience than for the unbeliever," said Frank E. Gaebelein. "The beauty of a Turner landscape or a Rembrandt still contains for him a double beauty—the hand of the artist and also the hand of a personal and loving God."

B. F. Kurzweg, in his book *The World That Is* (Concordia Publishing House), gave an excellent illustration of the difference between the Christian and non-Christian artist. "A Christian and his non-Christian friend are discussing a landscape painting. Both of them may express their impression that this painting reveals the beauties of God's creation. The non-Christian may see God in terms of the landscape. He finds God in what he sees. Accordingly, he sees something his mind has deduced. He sees a god, but not God. The Christian does not see God in terms of the landscape; he sees the landscape in terms of God. He does not deduce God from the painting. He has come to know God in the revelation of Christ. The picture he sees depicts the handiwork of the God he knows."

As Clyde S. Kilby, English professor at Wheaton College, says, "It has apparently not occurred to many Christians that they do not have a choice between imagination and no imagination, between creativity and no creativity, but that their choice lies between a good and a poor imagination, between worthy and unworthy creativity."

Sometimes parents, and consequently their children, will feel uncomfortable around great art because they have never taken the time to understand it. A thing is not necessarily evil or wrong because the looker or listener does not understand it. It's past time for us to set a standard with which we will be able to distinguish good and bad in the art with which we live.

Grant Reynard has written, "Christians will do well to spend more time in raising their level of appreciation. Art, whether that of the great masters or the humbler efforts of lesser talents, belongs to those things God has given us to enjoy. And in its truest integrity it exists for the glory of God.

"We need architecture that fittingly houses places of worship, music that worthily praises God the Father and brings men closer to God the Son, pictures on the walls of our home that, while not necessarily religious, are examples of good art. We need Christian artists of dedicated talent who will extend their horizons in humility and devotion to the true praise of the Giver of talent, who is best honored by the faithful use of his good gifts."

I have an artist friend who tithes his talents. He earns his living for his large family by doing commercial art, including animated television commercials. But Joseph DeVelasco also works for Christian companies that are unable to pay the enormous sums available in an advertising budget. "I'm giving some of my talent back to the Lord," Joe said. "It's what I have that's worth more than money to me—the greatest gift I can give to my Lord, next to my life. If children and teenagers are drawn toward the Savior through my art, I have been a good steward.

"My daughter has chosen a different creative form—
mime. She loves it and I think she's very good at it. I would
hope that she too will tithe her talent. She and my other kids
are part of the reason I'm so careful about how I use what the
Lord has given me."

As you search Scripture for principles to apply to the
raising of your children, you won't find one that tells of
your duty to introduce your child to his creative potentials.
Perhaps this omission shows that God wanted parents to
make this discovery for themselves, as they lead their
children through childhood. This leading most effectively
begins in the home. "Men and women may sometimes,"
said Rudyard Kipling, "after great effort, achieve a
creditable lie; but a house cannot say anything but the truth
of those who have lived in it."

Artistic creativity for the child is, of course, on a different
level than the creativity of the masters. Very few children
will have a talent that will be worldshaking, but this
doesn't excuse us from placing before children all the
opportunities possible to familiarize them with great art,
superior music, and creative literature.

In each of these areas there are two distinct avenues to
which you should give attention: that of allowing the child
full expression of his own in his childish way and that of
exposing him to great art so that his taste and discernment
are broadened.

CHOOSING ARTWORK
FOR YOUR CHILD'S ROOM

I heard a story about a family with five sons. Each son
grew up and went to sea, even though he had always lived in
an inland city and had seen the ocean only once before giving
his life to it. "Why?" the mother asked herself, and she had to
wait for years until one day her youngest son gave her the
answer.

"It's that painting," he pointed to the large painting of a
beautiful ship moving majestically through choppy seas. For
years that picture had hung above the living room couch.
Each son had grown up looking at it; each son had been
influenced by it.

Giving a child a love of pictures is the first step toward giving him an appreciation for art. Therefore he should be exposed to a wide variety in his home and especially his room.

You might even like to have a bulletin board for the child where he can display pictures of the seasons, special interest subjects of the moment, or the child's own colorful originals.

You will want some permanent pictures to which the child reacts positively. The preschool child likes single object paintings, ones that show happiness and movement, ones that elicit bright-color responses. He shies away from busy pictures with heavy shading. Anything that shows pain such as a realistic picture of Jesus on the cross could be more of a hindrance than a spiritual help to him.

There are so many good, low-cost reproductions available to the child that it is a shame to settle for works of second-rate artists. Your child should know about the pictures on his wall. He should feel free to express his feelings and questions about this story that is not told in words. Use good Christian artists, but don't limit your pictures to only those labeled religious. Your child just might love modern impressionistic art in which the artist's effect was airy and colorful rather than depressing.

"We discovered that our library loaned beautiful reproductions on a three-month basis, so our home always had one," said Dee. "I discovered that some pictures I loved when we chose them did not have lasting appeal. I was thrilled to take them back. Others I was almost willing to pay the overdue fine to keep for an extra week. That exposure certainly increased my understanding of art."

There are varying opinions about pictures of Jesus being placed in a child's room. While he is young, he should learn that Jesus is not Sallman's head of Christ. The problem could be resolved by having two pictures of Christ, two completely different representations, so that the child realizes that no one really knows what Jesus looks like. You might ask your child what he thinks Jesus looks like and have him draw his idea before the pictures are placed in his room.

In choosing a picture of Christ for the child's room, the

parent should be sure that Christ looks happy and strong. The painting "Follow Me" is an unusually good choice because Jesus is portrayed as a strong man, smiling as he confidently leads children into the smoke-stacked city where there is work for them to do.

Parents might enjoy planning a picture tour through their own and their friends' homes so that children could see how different pictures fit the personalities of different rooms. The parents might tell why they chose this one for the den and another for the bedroom.

You'll also want to introduce your child to the art galleries in your area. Children are going to live with art for the rest of their lives. How they view it, what joy and understanding they gather from it, will be largely determined by the parent in the early years of the youngster's life.

A SPLASH OF PAINT— THE CHILD'S INTRODUCTION

My mother was a first-thing-my-child-did saver. I have a rather humorous baby book that contains my first fingernail clippings and a small tissue with brownish spots labeled, "The first time Marlene cut herself." And I also have my first picture in which the figure was recognizable—a bunny. Mother must have helped me put a cotton tail on the creature and for the past three decades my bunny has reminded me that my mother cared about my earliest splashes of color.

A child may find his experimentation in art an introduction to himself. Here he is able to express himself in a way that only he can. What he puts on paper in front of him is right—at least it's right to him, no matter what the faulty perspective or weird color combination.

He doesn't ask that what he has drawn or painted be considered great art. He just wants it to be an expression of his own experience at that moment, a pleasant activity, and usually nothing more. Through painting the child expresses his knowledge of the things in his world and his relationship to them. What is important to him at this moment, he will draw.

A preschool boy drew nothing but airplanes. He loved them and told everyone that someday he would pilot a plane just like the ones he had drawn. His parents wanted him to try drawing different things and suggested he draw their home for a change. He complied. He drew a square box house with an airplane on the roof.

Through painting or coloring, a child can inform the adult world of his likes and dislikes, what has meaning to him, and what dictates to a great extent how he reacts.

The child's world is chaotic. He must pull together the many loose ends to which he has just been exposed into one meaningful whole if he is to become a balanced person. Through the many expressions available to the child, as he paints or makes from a mound of clay something that has a definite meaning to him, he is telling his parents just how he thinks, feels, and sees.

One of the most devastating, revealing exhibits of children's drawings I ever saw was entitled, "I Never Saw a Butterfly Again." It was a collection that violated all of the happy growth we want to see happen in our child; it consisted of drawings hidden and/or smuggled from Hitler's death camps. What those pictures said about life on the edge of murder, people's inhumanity to people— children as well as adults—children's emotional experiences, and perceptions of the concentration camp spoke volumes to the adults there. They knew those works had to be saved, for they told the story of what must never happen again—a story without a single word. One child had drawn a picture and over it smeared line after line of heavy black color until little was left but an ugly hole covering everything else on the sheet.

Art for your child may well be his friend that allows him to express emotions—hopefully happy ones—when there are no words that can say what he feels.

The young child armed with a crayon and lots of white paper may be training himself for a creative future. Little is as valuable to his self-formation as this continuous outpouring of the forms and shapes that lie within him. Parents are the ones who teach or at least structure the first art lessons.

In their book *Creative and Mental Growth* (The Macmillan Company), Viktor Lowenfeld and W. Lambert Brittain say that what happens within the child you are encouraging "may well mean the difference between a flexible creative human being and one who, in spite of all learning, will not be able to apply it, will lack inner resources, and will have difficulty in her relationship to the environment. Because perceiving, thinking, and feeling are equally stressed in any creative process, art may well provide that necessary balance for the child's intellect and his emotions."

Art is more than an introspective expression by a child who cares only about his immediate world. Your child may never be an artist, but he will have the excitement of doing "art." Because he has participated in the process, he will more readily understand as he grows older what others are saying through art. How wise you are to help your child find freedom and creativity in himself, expanding his or her view to include others who express themselves differently. If he is to become an individual because of his unique qualities, he must be willing to see these same qualities in others.

Art also teaches your child about organization. What was acceptable scribbling at three must gain some purpose at seven. A child learns that although his ideas and his imagination can run free, there is a pattern to things, a beauty to be found in the world of expression only when the rules of art are followed. If his art is to have meaning, he must say something to others as well as to himself. This pattern of meaningfulness will carry over into other areas of his life, so that what began as random wandering of a crayon develops into expression that is understood by the group. This understanding in turn develops into the ability to cooperate with others in the world today.

Not only will your child find an introduction to himself in art, but you'll find keys to his self expressed there also. There is no better way for you to know your child than through his creative work. It's not so much your duty to teach your child about art as it is to encourage him in the process, to be proud of him and to show him that he is a person of worth. In fact, it might be difficult for you to teach, to put limits on your child's art without ruining his creative spirit, for the uncoerced child seems to respond most positively to the creative process. Teaching art is unnecessary at these early ages.

Parents can become loving bystanders in the child's artistic development and the love they give is the most important part of the process.

Encouragement, too, plays a large part, but participation in the process by parents often leads to the stifling of the child's undeveloped attempts. His enthusiasm collapses under an adult's more skilled portrayal. For instance, if a child asked for help in drawing his brown dog, the parent might aid him by asking, "What do you feel when you pet your dog? Now draw what you feel." This is much more helpful than if the parent took the pencil and drew a four-footed animal for him. The child can draw his responses to your questions, but he will never be able to successfully draw a dog as well as his parents can. Would you want him to? His life isn't a pattern following his parents as a carbon would copy; rather his life is an experiment in living, all his very own.

David had just finished his map of Michigan, a project for a third-grade class. He showed it to me, and it was obvious that he was terribly proud of it. I forgot all about my caring for my nephew and saw only the map—a rather flat enlargement of a map in his book, a perfectly obvious shape of Michigan, nothing wrong with it at all. But I used my adult eyes. "What that map needs," I said, "is something to make it unique, exciting." He looked crushed. "Here. I'll show you," and off I went into the yard to pick the tiny tops off some of the evergreen bushes. In my enthusiasm over the map of Michigan, I showed David how he could use white glue and attach these little "trees" to the map to show where the forested areas were. What a great idea; his map would be the envy of every kid in his class. I sat back and waited for his praise and his rush out the door to pick additional trees. Instead, he was crushed. He nodded that he understood and stuck his map back into the book. I have a feeling I ruined that map for him forever. It wasn't good enough for an adult. I hadn't praised his efforts. What a dumb thing to do! I suppose all of us who love kids have to remember that although the rules make sense, they are difficult to follow. We fail, and we do better next time. There is no doubt that I will behave differently when David shows me his next work of art—if he ever dares.

Again from the book *Creative and Mental Growth* comes some more helpful advice. I would have been smart to remember it. "Avoid criticism after their work has been finished. . . . Too much emphasis on the final product may stress it beyond its significance. We must remember that the child does not engage in creative activities to produce pictures, but to express himself. We must also remember that the art expression of the child is not aimed at producing artists. Rather it serves the child as an important means to his growth, regardless of whether we consider the creative product 'beautiful' or 'ugly.' "

Paul Smith agreed and added in his book *Creativity, an Examination of the Creative Process*, "Few things are more detrimental to a child's creative development than to tell him that his work doesn't look like something, or that it isn't in proportion, or doesn't have the right color. During the early years, free trial-and-error, exploration and observation of the world are essential for subsequent growth."

Don't examine your child's work too closely. Instead enjoy it as a natural, honest, and exuberant expression of the awareness your child has of himself and his world. His work expresses the essence of things, while we adults strive so hard for spontaneity. There is not much difference between the adult's and child's creative process, but the adult works consciously to be creative while the child's work is naturally his and his alone.

Children go through several main stages of artistic development, but they can't be put into developmental niches because the stages overlap. What they draw one day will not be repeated the next. What and how the child draws depends on his health and past experiences as well as his age. Until the age of three or four the movements of the child are merely kinesthetic or muscular. This is the time for unidentified scribbling. He is just manipulating material by moving the brush over the paint to see how it feels.

The beginning scribbler will draw with disorderly abandon, progress to the circle, and finally to longitudinal strokes.

Later a child will begin to label what he has done so that although his masterpiece has no recognizable form, he can tell the adult what he had in mind. These periods can be identified in the three-to-five-year-old child. He will draw the things that are important to him, and the most important thing is himself. "I" and "my" are the keys because he is learning how he fits into the world. Space, proportion, and color are not important.

In the third stage, organization, the child begins with a sky and baseline and is not really concerned with things as they are. For instance, he may show both the inside and the outside of a house on the same drawing, or the top and side view of a table on the same picture. He gathers increased awareness of things but has no perspective. He will delight in design and repetition. His scribbling, in addition to being a release and a source of enjoyment, will in its maturing expressions help the child gain coordination and understanding of his environment and of himself.

DON'T LIST FOR PARENTS

These ten don'ts will serve as guidelines for what not to do when you are dealing with your child and his splashes of color.

1. Don't do your child's art for him. Give him the opportunity to develop his own creativity without imposing your rules on him.

2. Don't give him coloring books that will cramp his creativity within adult-drawn lines; rather, let him work out his own images and impressions. In this same area, discourage his tracing or copying work that has been done by someone else.

3. Don't get too excited about the final product. This is not the important thing. Although it is an expression of the child at that exact time, the next hour it might not be.

4. Don't correct your child's art. If his perspective is

wrong, he knows it. As his hand becomes more trained to produce what his eyes see, he will be able to correct his own work if he wants to. To make corrections now would simply be saying that he's wrong and he and his piece are not worth quite as much as they would be if the picture had been drawn a different way. The child's art, like that of the modern artist, does not have to be beautiful. Creation does not necessarily mean the creation of beauty.

Expect to see some pain, some ugliness, in your child's art if what he is drawing truly comes from within him. It is his heritage as a member of the family of people. As a parent you must guide him into all truth, accepting his imperfections, leading him when he is ready to find the God of perfection.

5. Don't tell your child what he may or may not draw. Allow him to make his own decisions and then accept whatever he does as an outpouring of himself.

6. Don't compare his art with that of his peers.

7. Don't always expect an explanation of a picture he has drawn. Not all pictures have to look like or be anything. To a young child, art is no more than line, shape, texture, color. It is not picture. But aren't these the qualities a mature artist strives for? To the child art is emotional. He really feels it; he really enjoys it. If the child offers no explanation of his representation, let it go at that. It is his work, finished, and that is the important thing to him.

8. Don't expect to see every piece of art your child produces. As he gets older, he may resent this intrusion into his private thoughts. What he creates may be so personal that it would lose its value to him were he to share it with anyone, even someone he loves.

9. Don't show the child's art to those outside the family. Of course, you can enlarge the term family to include those you know your child would like you to share with. His work is an expression of himself and you don't want him to find in it a vehicle for merely showing off.

10. Don't overpraise his work. If it doesn't look like what he intended, he knows it. No amount of praise is going to make him feel any more accomplished and it may serve to embarrass rather than encourage him. He might also feel

that if the imperfect drawing is so excellent in his parents'
eyes, he doesn't have to try harder to achieve perfection.

DO LIST FOR PARENTS

Here are guidelines for what to do when you are dealing
with your child and his splashes of color.

1. Encourage your child. Perhaps a bulletin board in the
kitchen or the child's room could be used to show whatever
pictures he or she would like placed there.

2. Make sure your child has the supplies he needs to
experiment in many different artistic ventures. Be willing
to put up with the mess the child is bound to make.

3. Make sure to provide the time your child needs to
dabble.

4. Help your child respect what he has drawn as well as
the expressions that others make.

5. Appreciate your child's art for its own sake.
Recognize it for what it is rather than for what you hope it will
be or what it could be with a few changes imposed.

6. Let the child experiment so that he will develop a style
all his own. Don't make value judgments on these creative
streaks; let him decide in what areas he feels most at home.

7. Recognize that what may mean a lot to you because
your child made it may mean nothing to the child after he
has had a good time doing it. Don't expect him always to
see his work as anything of value, for no sooner has it been
completed than he is a different person who would do the
same thing in a different way, were he to do it again.

8. Make only general remarks about the finished
product.

9. If your child has a name for his picture, write it on the
sheet. Children's thinking is unique and their titles for their
pictures tell as much about their development as the
pictures themselves.

10. Let the child know that you have respect for him as a
person. His work is done in a way that no one else could
have done it. As he becomes more sure of his place in the
world, he will understand more completely how wonderfully
and fearfully his creative God made him.

COLORING BOOK?

The pictures might be interesting and very cleverly done from the adult's standpoint, but to a child the coloring book cannot help but lead him to a failure experience. He can see in his mind how a dog ought to look; he puts this thought on the paper. To him it is a freedom; he has created his own impression. But then he is exposed to the dog's picture in a coloring book. The nose is right, the tail is erect. The dog looks a lot more like the child's mind-picture than his own, so he concludes he can't draw.

Naturally he can't draw, when compared to adult standards of coloring books, but this is no reason to stunt him creatively or to curb his enthusiasm.

In *Creative and Mental Growth,* Lowenfeld and Brittain back this up by saying, "It has been revealed by experimentation and research that more than half of all children exposed to coloring books lose their creativeness and their independence of expression and become rigid and dependent."

Try an experiment with your own young child. Give him a large sheet of paper and ask him to draw a bird or dog. Later the same day, give him a coloring book with a picture representing the same thing you asked him to draw. Complete the experiment before you go to bed by asking him to draw the object again. Compare the first and third pictures. Which is more creative? In nearly half of the children taking this type of test, the first picture will be the more creative.

Why? In a coloring book he must just rework the emotion portrayed by the artist in the picture. There is no opportunity for him to relieve himself of his own tensions by creating the drawn object to correspond to the mood. A child becomes inflexible as he works with a line drawing.

Coloring books don't "promote skills and discipline," say Lowenfeld and Brittain, "because the child's urge for perfection grows out of his own desire for expression. . . . It conditions the child to adult concepts which he cannot produce alone, and which therefore frustrate his own creative ambitions."

We may find a possible defense for the coloring book for

the older child. It allows the child the opportunity to experiment in color within a well-drawn framework.

In the second and third grades when a child begins to work more and more with crayons, he needs to color one over the other, shading and blending and making new colors. He can see the need for this in a ready-drawn picture more than he can in his own representation.

MATERIALS YOUR CHILD WILL NEED

Though they are expensive, the materials a child will work with are worth their price. What might be viewed as just wasted scribbling must be seen rather as a developing activity, and the materials will lead the child toward fuller development.

Many artists would discourage the use of crayons and pencils in favor of paint for small children. With a paint brush in their hands, children can feel bright and free and unique because the paint with which they are working feels just this same way.

If crayons are to be used, select a heavy, thick set with a high wax content.

As the child grows older, he will like colored pencils to illustrate some of the projects he will have for school. If he is using watercolor, make sure it is a good set rather than the cheaper, dull-colored ones often sold for children. I always had colored pencils that would turn to watercolor paint when I added a bit of water to the finished product. They were difficult to handle, but they gave me both consistencies for the price of one.

Other materials, clay or plasticine, thin metal strips, plastic paints, charcoal, plaster of Paris, and soap that can be carved are interesting textures with which your child should be familiar.

"I think paper made the difference for me," said Diane. "I discovered that special papers made my finished product look so much more professional. When I would bring in my fourth-grade projects on watercolor paper, for example, the teacher would rave about them. I think I got all those strokes because my paper made my work look better than the other kids: That actually contributed to my decision to stay in the fine arts."

Paper is important. Because the child is using different types of paints and colors, a variety of paper textures will be needed. If the child is to use these creative materials effectively, you'll have to make sure the experience will be as successful as possible.

Success often depends on paper. Watercolor paper is made to have color spread over it in unique ways. For third or fourth graders this paper can make a difference in their attitudes toward their work. Heavy posterboard is good for tempera or crayons. Just ordinary good grade paper will do for the bulk of their work. It's a good idea to keep textured and nonabsorbent paper, as well as a good selection of colored construction paper, on hand at all times.

"My mother claimed she wasn't an artist," Jerry said. "But she certainly had an appreciation for those who could draw. I remember one day when she needed a boat for a flannelgraph story she was giving the next Sunday. She locked herself in the kitchen and sang 'Row, row, row my boat' for about an hour. She came out with a beautifully drawn boat. She didn't tell us for several days that she had traced it. Whenever we teased her about it, she would simply smile and say, 'Let me float my boat.'

"She wanted her children to be artistic, but because she didn't think she was herself, she didn't know how to guide us. So on Saturdays she would go to the art supply store in our city and read labels and see what was available. One time she came home with flocked paper, the first we had ever seen. Another time she discovered glitter. And then there was the day that we got white paste that didn't show when it dried.

"No, her kids didn't turn out to be artists, but we're both in creative fields. I suspect we owe the credit to our 'uncreative' mother and her excitement over the discovery of new ways to help us put our expressions on paper."

An added dimension to the child's art experience could be collage, a creative expression that uses pieces of many different things to create an impression, a total effect. For instance, the child may want to pin different buttons onto an old board. Deciding on a design is definitely an artistic experience for the child. For this type of thing, it is a wise parent who keeps a box of throwaways the child might be able to use: a broken zipper, egg shells, Christmas cards, empty spools, anything that will stimulate the child's thinking and make him take off imaginatively on his own.

WOULD THIS WORK IN YOUR HOME?

Don't you dare just copy my ideas! These are to get you started, but your own ideas will be so much better because they will be perfectly wedded to your situation—your youngsters, your community. Have fun! For children, that's what creativity is all about.

1. Work with your child in making a peep box that will illustrate something he is studying in Sunday school or school. The box would not be difficult to work with because the top is open. This type of three-dimensional art combines working with construction paper and with real objects he might get from your collage box.

2. Suggest your child make some toys of his own. Brads will give hand-drawn animals movable heads and legs. Cork could also be used to form the bodies and faces of zoo animals. Burned matchsticks might be used for feet while pipecleaners or paper will serve for the tail or ears. For the small child there are pinwheels or birds that fly on the ends of string. Would your children enjoy designing their own kites and painting on them their coat of arms or their own special insignia?

3. The whole family could work together to present a finger play. Inked faces on the fingers and tiny paper costumes give each finger puppet his personality. Children might enjoy playing Zacchaeus and Jesus for their parents during family devotional times. This small theater production takes nothing more than a box, a paper tree, and a little applied imagination.

4. Children love to work with clay. Yours might enjoy working on a complete manger scene. A box could be the stable. Many clays harden when they have been exposed to

air. The dried finished product can be painted. This might form the basis for a missionary project which, when finished, would be given to a retirement home or to a child the family knows who is spending the Christmas holiday in the hospital.

5. Finger painting can be fun for the whole family. It involves experimenting with color, texture, and movement. As the child expresses his feelings in this way, he will also be relaxing his tensions.

6. A frieze, or border, around their room could be made by your children. The border could depict a Bible story, fairy tale, or story of their lives. As they treat this as a continuous project, the children will take pleasure in watching the line of pictures grow.

7. Because young children are often fascinated with faces, the family might plan a portrait party in which each member tries to caricature one of the others. This same idea could be enlarged as elementary children present not only the picture, but also a written description.

8. Start with a potato. One that is left to sprout can become a potato plant that the child can watch grow. This will also work with a lima bean that has been placed on a piece of damp cotton. He could make a vase for this vegetable plant. "Potato people" are easily fashioned by using the eyes of the plant to emphasize facial features. Outline pictures can be cut from a potato by placing a picture on an open-cut half of the potato and trimming the white potato down around the outline. The raised part may be used for block printing. Simply dip the raised part in paint or on an inked stamp pad and press the raised section on paper. The block print can be used to make the child's personalized stationery—just perfect for writing thank-you letters to relatives.

9. For soap painting, make a thick paste of real soap flakes or beads (not detergent). Then brush the picture onto dark paper with fingers or paintbrush. Colored soap beads add to the effect.

10. Teach your child to feel; then what he has felt will be more adequately transferred to paper. Cut holes on the sides of a box for the child's hands. Through a third hole in

the rear, a second child can place all sorts of "feeling things" such as velvet, sandpaper, a balloon, for his partner to feel and guess the substance's identity. One college graduate admitted years after she was out of school, "I was twenty before I ever really felt the petals of a rose."

11. A lot can be done with waxed paper and an iron. Keep the iron on low heat and melt pieces of waxed crayon between two sheets of waxed paper. The crayons will spread into wonderful shapes and new colors. A mother might like to decorate her child's room with these designs for a stained glass effect at the window. A father might help his child use this process to preserve the color of fall leaves.

12. Put dots on a paper, any size and in any position. Then have your children connect them with lines, and from the lines envision a picture in them. This same picture process can be done using cloud formations.

13. Make the child aware of shapes in shadows. A whole new world of black and white controllable "monsters" come alive as children move their hands to make shadows. A young girl discovered shadows. "I think one of the times I will remember forever happened after all the other children had been put to bed. My father came into my room and showed me how to make an eagle by fanning my hands and using my thumbs for the bird's head. The bright spot on the wall where the street light shone was never the same after that. It became a circus, a farm, a science fiction movie, anything I wanted it to be with my hands."

14. Family art shows are successful only if everyone submits something. No prizes should be given, but the family could prepare something in secret, and on the given day the display could be held on a washline stretched across the living room. A permanent display wall could be made by stretching burlap over a large board. This is encouraging to the child; he knows he is appreciated and he sees his work as part of the group contribution. An art show shouldn't be limited to paints. Collages or wire sculpture are other possibilities.

4

STEP FROM
CREATIVE SPEECH
TO CREATIVE WRITING

Andy Botts

"I GREW up in a churchy situation," Judy said. "I had almost no personal contact with the world. I was popular in high school, but it was with the Christian kids, the ones in the Bible club. Every need I had was satisfied within the context of the church.

"Now in my community and in the adult groups at my children's school I am with predominantly unsaved people—fine, nice, upstanding people who need to see Christ in action. But I freeze. I haven't got a thing to say to them. I don't know how to make small talk.

"Not only do I feel uncomfortable and inferior, but I'm sure they feel this alienation and react negatively to it. But what can I do now?"

Too many of us echo at least part of Judy's problem. And perhaps one thing we can do is make certain the children who touch our lives do not face the same problem. If this whole Christian thing works, we'd better be able to open our mouths and our pens to those outside our safe, agreeing-with-us circle.

The command to effectively communicate the message that he has given his people is inherent in Christ's injunction to go, to teach. No other age has utilized communication to the extent that the twentieth century has.

With radio and television millions of people can be influenced by a single voice. Whereas books were a luxury afforded by the wealthy few not so many years ago, they are now available in every description, many without cost, almost all within the price of our salary limitations.

And yet we are falling behind in the race to win the world's people through the printed page. We are not growing writers.

Christian publishing companies are searching for writers who will appeal with a superior style to a world that is now well aware of the difference between good and mediocre literature.

The vice president of one of the largest evangelical mission boards said, "We would like to put out a better magazine. We beg our missionaries for material, and when it comes in it is in such poor, labored form that we either can't use it at all or it must be completely rewritten."

What about the spoken word? Surely here Christians can

do much better. Who among us can't talk?

Well, me for one. John lives next door alone. This sixty-year-old man enjoys spending evening hours at our home playing games, eating something gooey and fattening, sharing what happened in our respective days. I kept waiting for the right moment to talk to him about God. I waited for months. I'm usually quite comfortable sharing my faith, but John lives forty steps from my front door. Things could be very difficult if I hurt him or made him feel uncomfortable.

Finally John spoke up for me. "You leave every Sunday morning, I see. Are you going to church? Are you Christians? I thought you might be. Maybe I could ride along some Sunday."

So much for all my waiting!

We have the message. We know the value of that message, but, sadly, we have formed writing and speaking patterns that often make us unable to communicate it. And we are passing these negative patterns on to our children.

It's sad when those I wish to share God with have to bring the subject up to me! If I freeze, the message I have to share freezes with me.

If we look at Christ's example, we can see how he worked effectively on all levels. Within his group of friends, he taught and lived freely. But he wasn't uncomfortable, either, in the houses of the publicans, where the upper-class Roman social graces were emulated. He knew Jewish customs and social laws and was able to condemn Simon for not making proper use of them.

How Christ communicated! Though he never advocated Christians being a part of the world, he didn't shun participation in the world of his day. He was aware and he used this awareness. He participated in the fun and parties—the marriage feast at Cana. His language was colorful—"You generation of vipers!" He never stood on the outside looking in. Involvement, awareness, wholeness! These are key words that should be descriptive of Christians today.

Marc grew up in a home where he heard verb forms and tenses used correctly. You should hear him when he's talking with an adult he wants to impress—not a "them" or "those," out of place! But when he's with his friends, his language is an English teacher's nightmare. "All my friends talk like that," he explained when I teased him about his second language. "And as long as I know what's right, who cares?"

But last week, he let an "ain't" slip in the wrong group and he looked around sheepishly. "My friends!" he explained. "I'm just talking the way I hear."

Marc's an adult; he realizes the importance of knowing the correct way to speak. And he's just realizing something every parent already knows. Kids will talk the way they hear us talk at home. Poor English is limiting.

"I'll share the message and that's all that matters. God will overlook my rough spots." Will he, when the Joneses down the street won't? Our God is not second rate and we should do everything we can to be first-rate representatives of his message—in our lives and in our conversation. Isn't it proclaiming a sloppy Christianity when we don't make a conscious effort to correct an ain't-laden vocabulary?

This doesn't for a moment mean that the Lord can't use or doesn't use people who are not polished but are yielded to him. God can work through any Christian who is willing to let him. But how often does a Christian offend because his witness isn't all that—with God's help and an English book—it could be?

Our children will speak the way we speak. If they see our concern about our language and hear us working to make it as perfect as possible, they will follow the same pattern.

"You know how I got through English tests?" Jeanette asked. "I would read the sentences in my head and fill in the blanks with the word that sounded right. I got almost straight A's without knowing many of the rules. The wrong way was never used in my home, and although I couldn't tell you why one word was right and the other was wrong, I could almost always pick the right word."

Another difficulty we often have in communicating the gospel aloud or in writing lies in our use of a specialized vocabulary that is inflicted upon our youngsters even before they enter school. God is love, power in the blood, redeemed how I love to proclaim it, I'm so happy in Jesus; and on and on the phrases go.

One Sunday school teacher suggested a solution. "I was working with a class of unchurched primary boys and girls during Bible school and found it necessary for the first time to consider the basis of every word I used. I went home and made a long list of the terms that are used so often by Christians, some of them terms that had lost any personal meaning for me through overuse.

"Under the simple word 'love' that I used so glibly, I made myself write a hundred words to explain what it meant to me and how I would define it in a culture where there was no such word. I was surprised how much more vivid and meaningful my own acceptance of Christianity became and how much better I was able to teach my class these basic lessons."

Another teacher included her class in her search for understanding. "One of the projects I worked on in my seventh grade Sunday school class was the writing of a dictionary. Words like 'glory,' 'righteousness,' 'eternity,' became something meaningful to them as they formulated their own meanings. In most of them a theologian could have most certainly seen holes and incomplete ideas, but the girls at this age understood what they had written and they could communicate it to their peers."

When a person can speak something in a form that is acceptable to him and to those around him, the next step is, naturally, to write it down. The exercise is word fun. It's creativity in one of the highest forms, for it uses imagination, verbalization, and vocabulary written in a form that is understandable to the reader.

The excitement of language must be discovered and cultivated in the home. Perhaps if the young generation were raised with a full respect for their imaginative powers, the effect on succeeding generations would be greater. The child who learns the power of his words, the fun of conversing, the beauty of something he has written, will be on his way to a successful life of fluent interaction. Words! How they can serve, when parents take the time and energy to help their child capture them!

As you think about language skills, focus first on the child's verbal beginnings—the babbling, questioning years in the young child's life. What might be the obstacles to creative language training in your home? Too often a parent doesn't see the need for this expansion in his own life and therefore he is blind to the need for it in his own child.

Another problem is apathy—it seems too much trouble to encourage the bubbly spontaneous vocabulary of the child. Instead, his word pictures are laughed at; his ideas are dismissed as immature; his powers of communication are squelched.

The child grows. When there is no tradition of talking together at meals, the child loses one of the best incentives or spurs toward interaction. "I'm a lawyer today," Tom said, "because I had to learn to defend what I said around our kitchen table. We four kids enjoyed sharing our ideas and working hard to make those ideas make sense. That training will stand me in good stead the rest of my life."

Conversation between parents who love God and a child who loves and will someday see his need for a personal acceptance is invaluable. Too many homes still operate on the autocratic principle that children should be seen and not heard, or its opposite—voices and clatter and noise, but no conversation taking place. What a shame. This is the time in their lives when they are completely free from adult clichés and the imposed ideas of others.

Only a child could announce, "I want to tell you something I just thunk." Or, explaining an accident she had just witnessed, "Car, bunny, bang. All broke." Or an explanation when he saw a Great Dane for the first time, "Look, is that woo-woo a horse?"

This is the period above all others in which our children must be heard if they are to speak—or write—with any significance in the years to come.

WORDS ARE MY COLORS

A child doesn't just decide one day that he has enough command of his language to put his thoughts on paper. But if his parents are wise and have trained the child in verbal skills, the child will grow up feeling that what he has to say can be said just as easily with a pencil as with his voice.

Writing, especially creative writing, starts with a good vocabulary. This vocabulary begins even before your child is able to talk. Since his understanding is far beyond his ability to articulate, you should use good English, simple and colorful words around him from the first. If he is exposed to goos and coos from adults rather than carefully spoken words, naturally he will progress more slowly toward good pronunciation and verbal proficiency. When the child is just beginning to talk, nearly every parent is willing and excited to spend long hours coaxing and helping him form syllables for himself. But as the child gets older, it is somehow more difficult to take the time really to appreciate the nonsense, the funny giggles, the endless questions with which the child bombards you. He is beginning to dabble in oral language, but he still needs intensive practice. Talk! Talk! Talk! Of the principles a parent should follow as he trains the child in pre-writing skills at home, none is more important than just letting the child talk.

When a child asks his long string of why's he is not so much searching for the answers to his questions as he is vying for your attention. He wants to listen and be listened to. It's so easy to forget that the child talks for the same reason anyone else talks—because he has something he thinks is important to say.

One family had a talking time. The daughter explained. "Every night, after the dishes were finished, my parents would encourage us to talk endlessly about anything and everything. Mother and Daddy set this time aside to give us their undivided attention. That's what I remember best. They were interested in what we had to say.

"Our parents were genuine about the whole conversational thing, and each of us kids knew they cared about what we had to say. It made us anxious to say all sorts of things that I don't think we would have said if we hadn't felt this freedom during our talk-time.

"When we started to school and got involved with other activities, we no longer had formal talk-time, but our parents still took the time to talk whenever the opportunity presented itself. There was never that age barrier between our parents and us and I think one of the reasons might be that we set up good communication lines that stayed standing all through our growing years."

This mother has a unique way of stimulating family talking. "In our house we have initiated a discussion box into which go all the questions for discussion at a family meeting each Friday night. Family night doesn't follow a pattern, but when there are questions in the box, we discuss them. In this way each of our children has an equal opportunity to talk about a subject he is interested in, and he knows he will have the support of his family in a give-take situation.

"I guess the box isn't really necessary, but when they write their questions, the children build enthusiasm for our times together on the weekend."

"I think I have the most complete baby book ever made," a mother said. "I have long since ceased to be nostalgic about the first baby tooth I pasted there, but I don't think I'll ever tire of reading the cute things my children said through those years. They had such a simple way of putting things together; their natural freshness and beauty never cease to amaze me. On a blustery January day my son, remembering the days in the summer when he was allowed outside without a shirt, asked, 'When can I go with this part 'ticking out?'

"Then there was the time when we talked to the new minister's wife. 'Oh, you've got the most beautiful, big brown cow eyes,' my daughter announced."

Parents should never try to correct the colorful language pictures of their children. Their phrases express what they feel in a way that they think is adequate, and it is so much more an expression of themselves than the word pictures offered by most adults.

For instance, a little girl looked at the dog's tail. "It's a paint brush, that's what it is—a squiggly paint brush." A three-year-old boy explained as he waddled outside, bundled in his winter clothing, "I'm all bandaged up." As she stared at the clouds, a little girl said, "They look like a wig for Grandma."

It is a wise adult who tries to place himself into the mind of his child once in a while. It's not always the quiet, peaceful, secure place adults like to think it is. If the adult could think just as a child might think, he would better be able to hold meaningful conversations with the child.

This is a more difficult task than it would at first appear. The child's life is filled with looking up at things that are bigger and more powerful than he. His is a world of selfishness expressed in terms of "my" and "mine." Fear is a real thing even to a young child. A child can fear deeply over such small things. "I think the earliest memory I have is of fear," an adult remembered. "I may have been two. As a doorstop, my mother used a heavy iron bulldog. I used to dream about that dog and he would grow to huge proportions and stand by the door growling, not allowing me to get out. When I asked mother to take it away, she wanted to know why, and I can remember that I was ashamed to tell her.

"That dog is an antique now, and unfortunately, since I know its value, I can't get rid of it! But it's not the doorstop on my bedroom door! Never! Four decades later I still remember my childhood fear."

The child's world is one of "No!" and very few reasons for the no. It's a world in which the child is supposed to accept his position without question, for after all, he is a child. But for most children, life is also very happy. To them the imaginary, the fantasy is as real as the coffee cup in the kitchen cupboard.

"I was in kindergarten when we moved from the country home that I loved so well into a second-story apartment on a city cobblestone street," a college student said. "Mother used to let me play outside, but there were few children my age on my block. I wanted to fly back to my home in the country where there were so many things to do, and then one day I flew. I remember it, and although I realize that I couldn't have flown, I can tell you about how it felt, how I accomplished it, and exactly how far I went. I just pulled up my legs and held onto them as tightly as I could. I didn't get very far off the ground and it took quite a bit of effort, but I did get from the beginning of the fence to the end of it. This is about twenty feet!"

It is not uncommon for the preschool child to conjure a playmate and adopt the play friend into his life as surely as if the figment were reality. A mother tells of her experience. "Since we lived in the country, Susan had no playmates. I was surprised to hear her talking to someone in her play house. The friend's name was Argot, and she had obviously misbehaved, because Susan was giving her a terrible scolding. I opened the door to the play house and found there was no one there but Susan. Realizing that the playmate was important to her, I decided to go along with it.

"I got Susan to introduce me to the girl and the three of us had tea. Thereafter, whenever Susan did something naughty and I'd begin to scold her, she would explain that it hadn't been she at all, but Argot who had been the guilty one. When she started to kindergarten and found real children with whom to play, Argot was forgotten."

The child's mind is not really so different from his parents'. He has the same emotions but on different levels. He's not just a little person; he's a person in his own right, a wonderful treasured someone, because he stays that person for such a short time.

The child should learn not only that what he has to say is important, but also that what others have to say can help to enrich his life. The parent will want to teach the child the worth of all people. This he will learn as he talks and listens to others talk, expressing his ideas and understanding the ideas of others.

Much of this give-and-take sharing is learned in the home. As your family talks together about decisions that are important to all of you, you are binding your family unit more closely together. Each person who takes part in the decision will feel that the decision is his. He belongs; he is important.

The home is the natural place to teach your child to be comfortable in conversation. In the home he has more in common with other people than he will have with any other group for the rest of his life. Family talk should just happen. Talk about everything: new books, a television program, the Sunday school lesson. Ideal! But of course, it rarely is. There are no rules and no greater imperatives in training a child in this area than just *talk*. Talking should never be forced, but should rather be conversational, free, and interesting.

If the group works out problems that affect all of you together, a decision can often be reached by consensus. The child should be allowed to take the lead in the discussion occasionally, to wander all over everywhere verbally if this is what pleases him. He may never cultivate a love for expression unless his family makes a conscious effort in that direction.

As a child learns to make conversation he will have a tool that will work well for him the rest of his life. As he increases his vocabulary and his feeling of verbal proficiency, he becomes a person who will be able to meet his fellowmen. He is in training (even before he has personally realized his need for salvation) to be the kind of person through whom Christ can work.

Without a command of his language, he will spend the rest of his life impoverished.

"A pianist may have the most beautiful tunes in his head," say Wilfred Funk and Norman Lewis in their book, *Thirty Days to a More Powerful Vocabulary,* "but if he has only five keys on his piano he will never get more than a fraction of these tunes out.

"Your words are your keys for your thoughts. And the more words you have at your command the deeper, clearer and more accurate will be your thinking. A command of English will not only improve the processes of your mind. It will give you assurance; build your self-confidence; lend color to your personality; increase your popularity. Your words are your personality. Your vocabulary is you."

A child's conversation is a wonderful thing; it should never be cut short. When there is a child in the family circle, the conversation shouldn't be monopolized by adults. Something in which he is interested should be interjected into the conversation. Encourage the restatement of the days' activities. You should ask good questions that will evoke sense impressions and vivid answers from your child. Let him know that you approve of his word pictures and play along with him in them.

And most important, as you talk with your child, enjoy

what is said. Your child will be able to tell when his conversation is truly accepted as a contribution or tolerated as a necessity.

WOULD THIS WORK IN YOUR HOME?

1. Perform actions such as the type used in the child's game, "Simon Says," and have each child give as many words as he can to describe what you're doing. Allow the child to make up words for each action as long as he can supply a fun definition to accompany his word.

2. Children love rhymes and enjoy making them. While mother and daughter are doing something around the house such as washing dishes, they could take turns making the first line of the couplet and the other could supply the rhyming second line.

3. Big words are fun, and parents might capitalize on this by suggesting a game in which the child tries to figure out the definitions of big words. The child could score one point for every syllable in the word he spells correctly.

4. Start a story and have the child tell the conclusion. The whole family could play this game with each contributing another paragraph. Be imaginative, parents, when you play this game, or your child just might outshine you!

5. Get picture books and let the child make up a story to go with the pictures. This same exercise could be used with the framed pictures in your house. The child might like to illustrate a story that has no pictures with some cut from magazines.

6. Establish a family court in which each member is allowed to bring problems and present his side in a particular situation.

7. Plan a reading party where family and friends bring their favorite story or poem to present to the group. This will give the child practice in public speaking and will also acquaint your children with the types of reading material that others enjoy.

8. Often daffy impromptu speeches are fun. Perhaps one child could give a talk on the "exciting life I lead on the string of my kite." Or, "my twin brother under my bed."

9. Have your child draw whatever comes to his mind when he hears words like "hairy" or "brilliant." Display the finished products on the family bulletin board.

10. Select two secret vocabulary words a week. Parents should make a conscious effort to overuse these words during that week, and it is the child's job to find what the new words are and, according to the context, what the meanings might be. The final step in this game would come when the child used the word correctly himself.

JUST TALK WRITTEN DOWN

Quite early your child will see that simple words can have lasting meanings if they are written. He will no doubt want to write before he is really able. A wise parent makes use of this urge and supplies him with paper on which to pretend he is writing.

"I recently got a birthday card from a five-year-old nursery school girl," a woman said. "It was composed of nothing more than her name written over and over on a large white sheet. She had colored some of the letters to make it an especially beautiful card."

An adult remembers his childhood. "My mother used to let us tell her stories about things that had happened to us during the day. If it had been an especially exciting day, she would write our story for us. I still have a collection of Sunday school stories we retold to her."

This is creative writing even though the child didn't really do the writing.

As children begin to write, they concentrate on familiar things and slowly they begin to draw from new emotions and ideas they are feeling.

They develop a happy mixture of familiar and wished-for characters. Rarely are the characters in a child's story dull. In every child there is a wonderful something just waiting to be placed on paper.

Careful! How very important are the attitudes he picks up from his parents when he begins to write. I can almost hear my mother saying, "That's wonderful," after reading almost everything I wrote. After the initial excitement she felt over my achievement, she would give me honest advice—a word change, a spelling correction, an idea I had missed. But oh, that spontaneous excitement! "I always copy my letters over," she explained one evening after finishing several pages to my Aunt Arro. "Words are important. I want to make sure I said exactly what I wanted to say; and," she added, "I wanted those words to look pretty, so she will enjoy reading my letter."

If his creativity is stifled as he begins to write, if he sees writing merely as a chore that has been assigned to him and has to be completed to earn a grade; if words mean nothing of beauty and everything of red marks for corrected spelling and grammar, your child may never desire to cultivate one of the most useful gifts God has given.

Parents must strive to instill a good attitude toward writing in his pre-writing years, for a dull or unthinking teacher can stunt his creativity, but she cannot crush it. The parents, with so many hours of the child's life entrusted to them, cannot only crush but can destroy creativity.

In his story writing the child has found a way to talk back. He can answer the adult world that has spent so many years saying no to him. He can release his tensions, for whatever he writes is his exclusively. In his stories he can manipulate his characters, and later, perhaps enjoy being manipulated by them. He can sass his mother; he can go walking in puddles, doing and saying anything he would like to do. His writing brings into the open much of what he is thinking and feeling.

Years ago, Clarice Madeleine Dixon said in her book *Keep Them Human*, "If we let art develop naturally from childhood on we would all be artists in some degree and capacity, and, from being able to express and to appreciate thoughts and feelings in color, sound, design, rhythm, etc., we would be freer, richer people, all of us.

"Little children have the ability to express themselves in any of these forms. Our job is to give them an opportunity."

And what if parents miss this opportunity? Is it too bold to suggest the future of Christianity in our land might rest on the ability of today's parents to train their children?

Training a child to write does more than teach him to put one word after another in an understandable sequence. It teaches him to use every bit of his creative power more positively and more completely than he does in any other means of expression. He is forced to think and to organize his thought. He must combine creativity with disciplined understanding of what he is saying. He is communicating with a world that is starved for words. And the results may be far reaching.

Ronald Gross and Judith Murphy included this illustration in their book *The Revolution in the Schools*. "I said to a friend of mine, a professor, recently, 'What kind of children arrive at the University?' . . . He said, 'They're all exactly the same . . . they come to me like samples from a mill. Not one can think for himself. I beg them not to serve back to me exactly what I have given to them. I challenge them sometimes with wrong statements to provoke at least some disagreement but even that won't work.' 'But,' I said, 'you must confess to about three percent originality.' 'One in a thousand,' he replied. 'One in a thousand.' "

What happens between the college years, when a professor can make such a terrible condemnation of his students, and the years before when children write so honestly? "The only thing wrong with children," wrote the authors of *Children's Letters to God*, Eric Marshall and Stuart Hample, "is that they grow up to be people. In the interim, they have a way of bringing us all up short with their directness, charm, curiosity, doubts, and reverence or lack of it."

A parent who is encouraging his child to write should pay at least as much attention to what the child is saying as he pays to correct spelling and punctuation. The child is thinking of what he is saying and not the mechanics behind the process. Little can dampen enthusiasm for a short story's completion more than flat criticism—when the only comment the parent can offer is, "Rhubarb isn't spelled that way."

Don't tell your child what to write. All too often the public school teacher will assign the child a subject in which he has no interest. This can be good training, but it doesn't have to happen at home.

"My mother never insisted that I write dutiful letters," a teenager related her experience. "I remember once after Christmas mother encouraged me to write a short story about the mittens my Aunt Nancy had given me. I entitled it, 'My new mittens and their first day in school.' It may have been incorrect etiquette to send this rather than a simple thank-you-for-the-mittens letter, but it meant a lot more to both of us this way."

Don't expect your child to finish writing everything he starts. He might lose interest. But what is important is the fact that he has begun writing and will write again. A college journalism major said, "When I was in third grade I decided that since my father was writing a book, I would too. I wrote about this large underground house that I had built for my family where they lived in safety while the war was going on above them. (I was preoccupied with the idea of bomb shelters). The story was peppered with 'I' and 'me,' but I was sure that it would someday be published. I never let mother read it, and after several weeks of writing secretly, I stopped because I just couldn't think of a way to end."

Make sure your child has enough material about which to write. He should always be kept aware of the world around him. Walks in the rain or a special night view of a falling star can add to his repertoire. And if, while he participates in these projects, he is encouraged to talk about them, his writing will become more relaxed and more an expression of himself.

WOULD THIS WORK IN YOUR HOME?

1. Keep a creative writing folder for each child that would contain his best work done at home and at school. So that he will have a sense of pride in the work he has done, include in the folder only those works that he and you agree are excellent.

2. Make a dictionary of words your child has learned, encouraging him to use his own terminology in formulating the definitions. It might be interesting to illustrate some of the words.

3. Simple games like "expansion" or any of its variations can be played for family fun. One word, a descriptive one,

is placed at the top of the page and the child sees how many others he can write that would be good synonyms or antonyms. Variation: How many words can he find to describe a noun?

4. Suggest your child write a story and from this make a "television" script. Pictures to go along with the story can be placed on long rolls of paper and then pulled past a window in a cardboard television set. If it is possible, the whole family might like to put the script on tape and use different voices for each character. (Preschoolers can talk/write their stories.)

5. In a family newspaper one member each week writes all the exciting things that have happened and these are placed in a newspaper scrapbook. It might be possible for a child to produce a neighborhood paper containing news about their pets and achievements at school, riddles, jokes, and perhaps a special interview each month. Reproduction is quite inexpensive.

Richard, the neighbor boy, and I did this in our neighborhood when we were in fourth grade. I think the first lead article was about my pet pigeon. We weren't interested in just the fun of writing news, though. We charged a penny a paper. Not a bad profit since my mother supplied all the paper and the hectograph.

6. In connection with a holiday like Thanksgiving, each family member could write a prayer. Since children often write in beautiful, unaffected free verse, they should be able to use some of this freshness to the glory of God.

7. Put an ink blob on a piece of paper and have the child make a list of the pictures that it brings to his mind.

8. Cut the original captions from cartoons and suggest the child think of new ones. Children might also enjoy drawing a picture to go with a caption from which the illustration has been cut.

9. Adopt a missionary family, preferably one with children the same ages as yours, and write a monthly newsletter to them.

10. Set words such as "plane" and "kite" at the top of a page and suggest your child list other words that have relationships to this first word.

5
THE SONG
IN MY CHILD

andy Botts

JOANN had been a mother only twelve weeks when she made the discovery. "Kathy was crying yesterday, but when I began to vacuum, she quit. When the cleaner's roar stopped, her crying began again. So I just set it by her crib and let it roar away. She loved the racket and was sleeping in no time. When she cried this afternoon, I tried it a second time and again she fell asleep."

A lost opportunity to begin to direct her child's love of sounds toward a love of music!

Music can lead our thoughts to God. Music lifts us from the finite world to the infinite, often giving us confidence and strength to face insurmountable tasks. Music joined with the spoken word reveals to us a truth far deeper and more significant than one form without the other. I remember going to Child Evangelism camp and learning to love the strong, majestic sounds of "A Mighty Fortress Is Our God." I must have been eight or nine, and as the difficult phrases were explained and we talked about them, I grew in my understanding of my God. Actually, from my perspective, my God got bigger. Music and words led me toward the understanding that God existed in more than love. He was strength, might, warrior, Lord.

The Christian with his voice lifted in praise to his Creator can worship deeply, significantly. While nature itself can become a song to God in its natural sounds—the rustle of leaves, the crack of thunder, a howl of high wind, the singing of the planets, the rhythmic breathing of a sleeping child—it is far more wonderful to realize that the believer can give a conscious song of love, awe, and praise to God.

We lovers of children can nurture this song in the child. We can give it depth and breadth; we can help the child reach his musical potential.

The child's musical education will begin with listening. It is possible that the musical atmosphere of the home is so important that if music is missing in the daily threads of life, it may make little difference how much time and money parents give to insure their children's musical education during their school years.

From about his eighteenth month until he is nearly eight years old, a child is excitingly free and creative with music. Then he usually begins to lose the melody which came to him so freely as a preschooler.

It's not known why a child loses his musical freedom in the first years of school. Perhaps as he hears the music of adults he finds his own inferior and unworthy of the public airing he has been giving it. Perhaps he finds himself afraid of his peer group's ill favor. They might laugh; they might not find what he has shared worthy of their praise. So rather than take the chance, he remains silent and stifles his creativity. Maybe the fault lies with parents who have pushed him too fast or offered him too little encouragement.

How very difficult to be a parent! Doesn't it seem practically impossible to give adequate attention to every important area of the child's development? I'm very glad Christian parents have the Holy Spirit as leader of their family circle. With his help parents can become sensitive to the possibilities for creativity within their children and work as best they can from there.

PRINCIPLES AND SUGGESTIONS

If a child is to develop a love for music, he must first hear it. Simple songs you sing to him while he is still in the cradle will help him associate music with love and security, all the things that are important to him.

Capitalize on your child's love of sound. Many children's toys can aid in the cultivation of rhythm and sound exploration. Such play things as a toy drum, whistle, or tambourine can stimulate the child's desire to play an instrument when he is old enough.

If possible, give your child access to a piano. As he drums on it, he can get an idea of what notes are. He can learn to play scales, and can easily see the difference between one note and another.

Mervin was just three when he suddenly discovered how to lift the cover over the piano keys. Instead of letting him just bang away, his mother taught him about the different garages. George lived in one and Adam in another, and so it went with the first letter of each garage corresponding to the name of the note. The child spent many hours finding Adam garages all over the keyboard. Although now as an adult, he appreciates piano music, he never did learn to play the piano. By the time his family could afford music lessons, he was already conditioned by his peer group to feel that only a sissy would play that instrument.

Parents must get excited about music. When the child sees in his parents a love for good music, he will hunt for the value in it for himself. You'll want to work with your young child so that at this time when his creative powers are running rampant, they may be expanded and channeled into areas in which the child has the ability for real expansion.

The home can be your child's musical palace. There he is free to throw his arms out and dance to the music as he feels it, or just sit and listen, or march or bang sticks on a kettle in time to a song in his head.

Leopold Stokowski in his book *Music for All of Us*, emphasizes the importance of the environment. "It is significant that music flows out of a child only when he is in a free environment," he wrote. "If his behavior is restricted in any way, music dies in him. Music is always associated with his own experiences in life—such as rhythmic motions—play in groups or by himself—rest periods when he is withdrawn from other children and his dream life wells up inside him. To a child music is never an isolated thing—but always a part of life."

There are two aspects to music education. In the first place, the child will want to participate in some musical expression. This could mean music lessons, even though the lessons will lead very few to be great or even good musicians. The point is that children should, if at all possible, be given the opportunity.

Second, every child should be taught how to listen to music. Parents can instill a love for the right kind of sounds. Music will stimulate the child's thoughts; rhythm will let the child feel beauty, motion, freedom.

Your child should be aware of many different types of music. The world in which he will play a part will mirror its life in its music—music sometimes filled with dissonance and abandonment of rules. Although the child must realize eventually that this musical picture for him as a Christian does not reflect his world, he should know about, and appreciate the skills involved in playing this type of music. He should grow to understand the despair of a world searching for a song without God, and with this understanding, he should learn to point them to that song.

In Calvin Miller's book *The Singer*, there are two songs in the world. One is sung by the World Hater and it binds and cripples those who hear and follow it. The other is sung by the Singer, the Christ figure. Through his singing his song, the world can be healed and freed. It is his song that we want our children to hear, and follow, and sing triumphantly over their own worlds.

Here, from *The Singer*, is an example to follow:

At last he sang!

*He threw the song against the
basalt canyon walls*

*It ricocheted in splendor,
and he remembered far before
that he had sung those very
canyons into being.*

*"Father-Spirit!" he shouted
at the desert sky, "I love you.
Ask of me anything you will
and I will do it all."*

*"Sing my ancient Star-
Song to the world"*

*"Father-Spirit, I will sing it,
in every country will I sing
it, till all the world you love can sing it."*

TRAINING YOUR CHILD TO HEAR

Sounds everywhere! Children love sounds, and they don't limit their appreciation to the commonly labeled "beautiful." You can have a lot to do with opening the wonderful world of sound to your child so that he will become an appreciative listener.

What would happen on a listening hike with your child? The object would be to find a new sound you had never heard before. You wouldn't have to know anything about music to be very aware of sound. Perhaps one day your child will say, "I think I would credit my interest in music today to those early walks in search of nature's musicians."

Listening ability is not automatic. A child must learn how to listen. Music can be a background to our activities—playing or working around the house, or even praying at church. But at those moments we are not really listening.

How can you train yourself and your child to sometimes put the music in first place? Listen to the music. That is what you are doing; remove it from the background and place it in the fore. It's not easy to just sit and listen. The music—stay with the music! Listen to it. Feel it. Anticipate it. It's a skill I've never learned. I first became aware of how much I missed of music after I sat through a piano and oboe concert in college. I just couldn't listen. I planned my next week's assignments. I played around with some couplets that fit the rhythm I was hearing. I even counted red dresses in the rows in front of me. My mind did useless things and it missed an opportunity to grow. My ears were retarded. I didn't really hear the music.

When I realize how careless I am about what I hear and the attention I give to the difficult job of really listening to music, I often think of Gladys. She has always had difficulty hearing. She said, "I remember as a child when hearing aids first came out. They were unsightly, bulky contraptions. The first time I went outside with one on, I heard the birds sing. For the first time! Think of it. It was wonderful. It was the moment I knew I would wear that aid forever, no matter how ugly it was. I would wear it even if I had to carry the heavy batteries around in a suitcase!"

The child will naturally prefer the music to which he has most often been exposed. If he is to appreciate the best music, it will require that he hear it many times, for good music is not digested or loved easily. Only after it has been heard often can the listener begin to feel the pattern of the whole wonderful composition in his mind.

"Why am I a musical person today?" says Frank E. Gaebelein. "Because of my home. Among my earliest memories is that of hearing my father and my oldest brother playing Beethoven's Fourth Symphony in a four-hand piano arrangement.

"Or I recall waking up on one of the Sunday mornings when my father was not preaching and hearing him play Mendelssohn. . . . My father and brother were not fine pianists, but they loved and played good music. Yes, musical education is impossible apart from the habitual hearing of greatness."

Children don't have to be bored by good music. If they have been exposed to music in their homes, they will be willing to expand their appreciation beyond the few songs or ditties they can easily master.

For many people, music is the most difficult of the arts, for unlike a painting, it is not a single tangible item that can be viewed from the same perspective again and again. In music, the listener's response must be fleeting because no sooner has one pattern been formed than another has begun.

Listening to music can be, for some, a difficult and tedious business. We have to pay careful attention to what is happening at this exact moment without forgetting what has gone before. Many people have never trained themselves to do this and are therefore bored with classical music, for example, because they can't find the pattern or links in the succession of sounds.

Even though a child might not be able to understand a certain piece at an early stage in his development, that doesn't mean that he shouldn't be exposed to it. Play it and play it often; play it just for his enjoyment.

The child's listening sphere is broadened as the communication medium expands. The FM radio offers excellent music almost any time of day. Many communities have a children's opera or puppet operetta sponsored by local clubs or the children's branch of public libraries.

If you follow through on this idea and actually take your children to a special opera they might enjoy, prepare them by reading the story to them several times before you attend.

A record player should be a household necessity. The choice of good children's records is growing, and among them are a number of sing-along and action games for rainy-day home activity.

Consider the records that teach Scripture by setting the words to easy-to-remember folk tunes. Here words and music work in harmony. Make certain that as children learn the music they also learn and understand the words. Many of these Scripture songs are written in King James English. They are beautiful, but perhaps difficult for both children and adults to understand.

Take, for example, one song that my husband and I learned at prayer meeting. The words include, "I will sing unto the Lord, for he hath triumphed gloriously: the horse and rider thrown into the sea." The pastor never explained the words, but each week we would all sing with gusto. The tune was great. One evening on the drive home, Jack and I talked about what the words meant. "It must be talking about some portion in Revelation," we concluded. "It's some hint of what is going to happen to the forces of evil when the Lord returns."

One day I checked with a friend who enjoys these songs. "No," Dean said. "That song comes from Exodus 15. Moses and the children of Israel sang it after the Lord had drowned the Egyptians in the Red Sea." Yes, great song. But not if I don't understand the meaning of the words I am singing.

Yes, great melody. But not if I don't take time to listen—really listen.

WOULD THIS WORK IN YOUR HOME?

1. School children could make and illustrate a "Favorite Songs" scrapbook. Music could be cut from old books that

are no longer in use or copied from a variety of books onto lined paper.

This illustration was given in a booklet, *How Children Can Be Creative*, released by the U.S. Department of Health, Education, and Welfare. "A Denver teacher played a recorded movement of Beethoven's Fifth Symphony for a group of fifth-graders. On large pieces of paper, they expressed their reactions to the music in color and form. If the music soared, so did their designs. If it was heavy they used dark colors with heavy blocks and forms.

"When it was bright, they used yellow and orange and pink with sharper, less massive designs. When one melody was heard over another, light colors and lines were drawn over darker and heavier designs. From this beginning the children created panels for their walls, a design for the back of their piano, a dance (with balloons and scarves), and a number of poems. All of these creative expressions grew out of listening to a masterpiece of music." (Authors: Wilhelmina Hill, Helen K. Mackintosh, and Arne Randall.)

2. Each chord, some artists would say, has a color. After the child has played several notes or listened to a short piece, encourage him to paint the colors he heard. This would make an excellent collage. His "sound in color" portrait would help him integrate what he has learned in these two related arts.

3. The child might enjoy listening to identify sounds from instrumental recordings. A culminating activity could be a trip to a concert so he could test his ability to identify instruments in a real life situation.

4. On a family listening night everyone might bring his favorite record. In addition to playing it for the group, the selector could tell why he chose this particular record. Primary and junior children might like to discuss why certain records appeal more than others.

5. Plan a situation in which the child could visit a song writer, pianist, or someone who is considered an authority in his area of music. As the guest tells the child what music means to him and shows him a bit of what can be done in his area of concentration, the child might generate some

enthusiasm for music lessons that will come later as he matures. If you like this idea but you're drawing a blank on a person to visit, ask yourself, "What about the musicians in my church?"

6. To show form in a more difficult piece, use choreography. One position or step could be used for the first section (A) and a second for the next (B). Should (A) be repeated, the child would once again go back to his original steps.

7. Ask the child to act what he feels as the music is playing. He will often do this without coaching, but if he knows his parents are excited about seeing how the music makes him feel, he will be freer and more expressive. (The parent shouldn't always watch the child as he dances. He needs time to be alone, to discover movement for himself.)

8. Make colorful streamers from crepe paper and allow the children to create beautiful designs in the air to light, flowing music. The same effect can be obtained with colorful scarves.

9. To aid the child in coordination, have him bounce large rubber balls or skip in time with a jump rope to more rhythmic pieces.

10. The child could write a story or poem while his favorite music is playing. Change the music and see if the tone of the story also changes. Adults as well as children find beauty and relief from tensions when they work with fingerpainting to a musical background.

11. As a help in picking out musical phrases and to make his listening more fun, have your child accent the endings of each bar by playing a triangle or finger cymbal.

12. Create Velcro music. I visited the Smiths' one evening and their two boys were having a great time creating their own music. Their mother had made a musical staff on a large piece of material. She had ping pong balls to which she had glued pieces of Velcro. Each boy could throw three balls at the staff. Of course, they would stick to the material. The boy would then play the chord he had hit on the piano. He got one point if he played it correctly and he got a second point if his chord was the better sounding one for that throw. Great fun, and also great argument as to

which boy had the best-sounding chords! As you might suspect, the chord that won was not always the one that was the most melodious.

13. A neighborhood group could learn orchestration while playing simple rhythm band instruments. The children, under adult supervision, could decide which instruments should play for each section of the song and why those particular instruments were the best at that point. Do you have family reunions? This band idea would be a great competition among families at a reunion. Each family and almost all members of each family would be able to participate.

CREATIVE INTERPRETATION

Most of the sounds that will intrigue your child will be associated with rhythm. The world hums and ticks. People walk, breathe with a rhythm. The buzz of the electric beater, the drip of a faucet, the tap of a foot—everything in our world has its own rhythm.

We share rhythm in common with all the plants and animals and people of the world, with all the stars and bodies in the universe. How we appreciate the rhythm in buildings, waves, music. Rhythm and movement are often inseparable.

Norma came to her mother and begged for an opportunity to dance for the company. Her father, a pastor, turned to the guests and suggested they let the five-year-old child dance just one song before she went to bed. Very simply Norma moved with the music in little skip-hops. Then her body would rise and fall with the music. For the child, it may not have been as natural as it would have been if she had danced for herself or her family alone, but it was a new experience for those watching. It was like seeing the musical score come alive and move gracefully over the lines and spaces.

A little child, natural and uninhibited, should be allowed to tell what music makes him feel in a way that is natural to him. He should respond spontaneously with inventive gestures and expressions as he feels with the music. Music comes alive to him; he has participated in its birth. With his movements he has found a new way of communicating, a beautiful and acceptable way. With his motions he makes the story tell itself; he relieves inner tensions or he puts into movement a symbol of something that had meaning to him in the past.

We want our children to learn that from within themselves can come beauty, creativity. And with what better instrument could he learn this than with his whole self?

My Instrument Is Me
Tapping feet,
Nodding heads,
Clapping hands,
Swaying backs,
Shrugging shoulders,
and
Walking, running, hopping,
Skipping, leaping, jumping,
Swimming, bending, stretching,
Galloping, cantering, bounding,
Pulling, punching, twisting,
Shaking, beating, splashing

Miriam E. Wilt, Professor Emeritus, Temple University

WOULD THIS WORK IN YOUR HOME?

1. Ask your child to imagine that he is caught inside a pretend box. In time to music, he should make his escape.

2. See how many different ways your child can think of to get from one line on the floor to another. He will begin with the conventional hopping, running, jumping, and progress to making up steps of his own.

3. By using a hoop or jump rope, the child can tell the story of a song in motions. Two children might enjoy working on this together.

4. Suggest the child pretend to be an inanimate object. "You are a teapot. How do you feel? How do you work?"

5. Play statue. In this game one child swings another

around and lets go of his arm. The child freezes in the position in which he falls. Other children might like to make suggestions as to what this "statue" should be named.

6. Set a record at an incorrect slow speed and have the child do slow motions to it. Change speeds until the child is doing "slap-stick" dancing.

7. Balance objects to music. The child might start with a book on his head and progress to a yardstick on his finger. As the child learns control and balance, he will become more graceful in his own movements.

8. In Japanese fashion, have the child move graceful hands in time to the music. If possible, take the child to see a Japanese woman doing these hand dances. Encourage your child to copy her.

9. Play musical follow-the-leader. The leader does different steps and motions all in time to the music.

A CHILD'S BEAUTIFUL NOISE

Most of us are too vicariously involved in music. To really enjoy, we must participate in making music. Singing is, of course, the most available type of music. Almost everyone has the ability to sing, maybe not in public, but for his own family enjoyment.

"I was working with a group of children in a Bible school in Vermont," a college student said. "I had planned to put a heavy stress on music. We began by singing our theme song. After the first times through in complete failure, I gave up hope that it would get better. I resorted to singing the few songs the children sang in Sunday school, but only a handful in that room of forty-five children, preschool through ninth grade, could carry a tune.

"I quizzed them about this. 'We don't have music in school,' they told me. 'There isn't much time in Sunday school since we have only a half hour together. No, I guess we don't sing much in our homes either because most of our parents work downtown and there just isn't time for singing.'

"These children, through lack of practice, were becoming non-singers. To be able to sing, they just had to sing. Sing everything, sing often. Toward the end of the two weeks, the children began to sing along with me. It was pretty much just a drone, but they were rising and falling as they should with the melody."

Every child can sing. There is no such thing as a monotone. With practice even children who have been labeled non-singers can learn to participate successfully. Adults must be careful with the labels they place on children. If a child is told that he can't sing or that he is a monotone, he will respond to your power of suggestion and his urge to sing will be stunted.

There are so many places where singing fits into family life. A girl told of her mother's unique idea. "Instead of asking me to do something around the house, mother would sing her requests. The two of us would make up the music for our singing conversation as we got the work done. Sometimes we would soar and find ourselves hanging on a wavering note while other times we would sing so low our voices would disappear. But there were many times in between when we sounded good, at least to us, and it made work fun."

Children can learn to sing harmony in the home and make group participation so much more enjoyable.

Begin the process by singing in rounds. Rounds give the feeling of harmony and they will help the children get used to carrying their own parts.

Parents aid their children in their vocal development in the same way they do other creative experiences—by giving the child the opportunity for doing.

What would happen, for example, if your family decided to make songs? They don't have to be masterpieces, but when they are finished, I suspect you'll feel there isn't a better collection anywhere than your homemade music. Start with Psalms.

During devotions read a Psalm twice and discuss it. Talk about the type of music that might be used with this Psalm, the emphasis the writer wanted, the important phrases that might bear repetition.

Gather around the piano and sing the words you heard. If ideas don't immediately flow, say the Psalm over together with as much emphasis as possible. When all your ideas are down on paper, sing through them. Even the youngest child can often suggest a tune that will go with the words. Pick out the notes on the piano—one finger will do. You might even go a step further and write the notes. That way in a night or two you can go back and look at your words and music again. The masterpiece might not seem quite as wonderful as it did at first, but then again, it might grow in its impact. If you still like the song, add it to your book of family songs. Sing it often. This is a fun idea that has enough appeal to hold the interest of your young children and enough sophistication to interest those who may be teenagers. And the only skills you need are reading, writing, and one-finger piano playing!

Radina Jensen, my roommate at Wheaton Graduate School, was a music major. She strongly believed that if there is a children's or junior choir in your church, you should make sure your children are participants. "In a junior choir," she said, "your child will be learning sight reading, essentials of singing, hymnology, and choir anthems, understanding worship, and developing musical taste. He should be acquiring a sense of responsibility in the ministry of music and receiving direct spiritual blessing while learning Scripture and doctrine."

Family sing-alongs are fun and children love them. But too often the songs are not chosen with the children in mind. Before the child can worship through a hymn, he has to understand the words.

Words have to be built around things with which he is concerned at this stage in his development. Primary children are often afraid of darkness and death. Songs about these things lead them to fear their God rather than love him. Music and words should breathe together; the child, when singing the songs honoring his God, should never sing without being aware of the meaning of the words. Then and only then will the music have its fullest intended impact on his life and understanding.

FOR EVERY CHILD—AN INSTRUMENT

Every child should have the opportunity to learn to play an instrument, whether it be a piano, violin, trumpet, or recorder.

Many schools still offer instruments for a small rental and in some areas the schools provide the instrument and group lessons free to the interested child.

Music lessons for children have been the subject of many jokes. It's difficult for the parent to listen to those first attempts—difficult, that is, if the parent hasn't realized the importance of music lessons.

Robert Elmore in a *Christianity Today* article, "The Place of Music in Christian Life" said, "Aside from the example of a consistent Christian life and a sound education, parents can give children few more lasting gifts than the opportunity to learn a musical instrument. And, contrary to American custom, let boys as well as girls have their chance at lessons; significantly enough, all the great composers have been men. Only a tiny minority of children will become professional musicians, and very few indeed will become highly accomplished amateurs. Talent is inevitably selective, and the gifted alone will continue. Yet even limited experience of making music is beneficial."

When Jim first got his trumpet he would often play outside during his practice session and all the neighborhood would hear his repetitive arrangement of "Cindy, Oh, Cindy." Before many years, he tired of his trumpet, but every once in awhile, now that he is a man, he'll go back to it and play "Cindy, Oh, Cindy" again and a little bit of his childhood comes back.

Sandra played for her own enjoyment, and to her, often a lonely and silent child, music was the outlet she needed. She would spend hours pounding out one melody after another as she found her way through a world that wouldn't accept her. And with each heavy beat the hurt was less. By the time she had finished playing she was at peace with herself and able once again to face her existence.

Children should have the opportunity to play in public. Sharing the arts is half the enjoyment. Often a church will have a band or orchestra in which a child can learn the beauty of his instrument in relation to the group. Without this group experience and approval, it will be difficult for your child to maintain his enthusiasm no matter how much stress is laid on lessons at home.

When a child has become interested in playing an

instrument, make every effort to help him. A time of day should be designated for practice. While your child might enjoy having you hear his finished piece, he will probably resent your listening to the entire process. The child shouldn't be forced to continue his lessons after he has reached his teens if he is no longer interested and his teacher agrees that he shows no outstanding talent in this direction. But in spite of his initial protest, the musical background is necessary for each child.

Every family has its little store of hilarious stories that lose something in the writing. One of ours involves Jim, my brother. "I think I always wanted to play an instrument," my mother would start the story. "I was determined to give you kids the musical education I never had. Jim couldn't have cared less, but I had always heard how great musicians thanked their mothers for insisting they practice, so I was determined.

"One day I heard what seemed to be a slight improvement from the music room where Jim was practicing. I went in to offer my congratulations, and there he was with his head down on the side of the piano, his eyes shut, slowly walking our cat up and down the keys. That did it. The cat could play better than my son."

Jim was about twelve when the cat event happened. He had been fighting to quit lessons for years, and mother finally agreed. "I realized," she said, "that I couldn't make him a musician. He had other gifts and talents that he needed to develop. But at least for the rest of his life he will be aware of the process that real musicians go through and he will better appreciate their success."

A well-qualified teacher who loves children is important. He should make the child's music fun as the child presents in his music a reflection of his inner self.

WOULD THIS WORK IN YOUR HOME?

1. The whole family might try its hand at making musical instruments. My mother used to make a big production out of playing the comb. She would put waxed paper over a comb and hum through it. She called it her

lived-through-the-Depression instrument. There are all sorts of other household things that could make music—or at least lots of fun noise. What could you do with sand paper, tin cans, chopsticks, rubber bands, balloons?

2. Perhaps each member of the family could do some research on the background of a hymn and this would lay the basis for a talking sing-along. Children below the age of ten might like to work with an older child or parent.

3. The family might form a recorder chorus. This instrument comes in a family of four: soprano, alto, tenor, bass. It is not terribly difficult to play. The wooden instrument has holes like a flute, but is played by blowing through one end. It has four tones and a two-octave range.

4. Allow each child to hear and see many different kinds of instruments being played. Perhaps the local music store would allow the child to try several types. This field trip could lead to the child's choosing an instrument with which she feels comfortable.

5. Encourage the child to experiment with different sounds he can make—making a scales with water-filled glasses or perhaps placing a piece of paper over the strings of the piano.

6. Let the child give answers to story problems on a drum. For instance, the parent might say, "You are very happy because you have just discovered a cave on our property. Let the drum tell how you feel." "You have just been told that we can't afford the puppy you counted on getting. How do you feel?"

7. Music games such as musical chairs and its variations are fun for a family get-together.

8. Form a kitchen symphony with homemade instruments the children have picked from the kitchen. The piano can hold all this noise together and the kitchen instrument can give the child a feeling of creativity and invention.

6
CREATIVE
DEVOTIONS

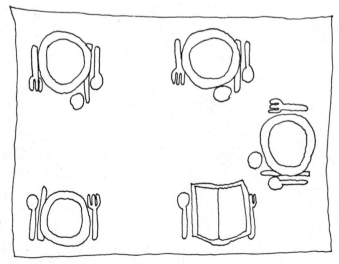

MY father was determined that we would have devotions every Sunday after church and before Sunday dinner. He would read long passages from the Bible and often give detailed explanations. It became a fight-for-survival time for my brother Jim and me. Would we last until dinner, or starve to death between Isaiah six and ten?

When we were older, Jim and I revolted against any kind of family devotions and occasionally during the middle years of our teens refused to stay at the table for them at all. I still often associate Bible reading with hunger pangs!

I guess because we never quite mastered the art of family devotions as I was growing up, I've watched my friends with interest. What makes their family devotions work?

For the Christian family in which parents have dedicated their lives and the lives of their children to the Lord, devotions become imperative. Family devotions, the time when the whole family gathers to worship God as a unit, should be just as much a part of the child's training as music lessons and elementary school. Religious instruction is that important time when the child's attitude toward his faith will be formed.

During family devotions, your child can listen and participate in a worship experience that is geared to his particular problems, his needs, and his family situation. Here he will learn to respect and believe what he has learned if he sees his lessons reflected in your actions.

What a responsibility this places on you as you depend on the Holy Spirit for help in guiding your child toward a positive lifetime decision. I find myself still struggling with devotions, that time alone with God or that time when our small family or our extended family—mother-in-law, Jack's brothers Marc and Gary, and Gary's wife and three small children—meet together to share about God. I carry the leftover baggage of my youth.

I remember once I was in charge of the extended family devotions for Christmas. Struggle, fuss, fret—it was a duty I wasn't sure I wanted. We ended up putting on a rather free-style family play. Some of the adults had written parts, and the preschool children participated by answering questions or telling small parts of the familiar

Jesus-is-come story. It was fun! It really was! And I felt I had studied the Bible with my family, gotten to know them better, and encouraged creative participation in Bible study in my nephews—reinforcing the positive tone that is encouraged in their home.

There was the family devotion in which we gave gifts to Jesus—actual little wrapped gifts of words or pictures that symbolized things we would do to show our love for him. Again, it was fun. I wanted to go back to my father and be a child again. "Hey, daddy. I have an idea. Let's do what the Risleys did. Let's draw pictures for Jesus. We could make devotions fun."

Devotions take time. It's often difficult to get ideas, to keep your child's interest. Strain your creativity as you make Christ and his message exciting to your youngster. God promised that the child who is exposed to his daily truth will have a bent to follow him for the rest of his life.

The home must be the primary teacher of religion, for it is here that the child is harbored during the most impressionable years of his life. You can teach in your home in a normal life situation. More and longer blocks of time may be spent on a lesson than in any other teaching situation.

Here lessons will have to be repeated and repeated, but your child knows he is loved. He will learn the lesson. And when he does, whoopie! You're there to see the results and to give positive reinforcement.

These unstructured learning, growing moments with God take place when they happen. Jim loved to climb trees. I think he still does. He was about four when a traveling brush salesman brought him to the door in his arms. Jim was red-faced, alternately rasping for breath and trying to cough. "I found him hanging from a limb. He had jumped or slipped and his scarf had caught on the branch. Lucky I came when I did," the salesman said. "He could have strangled to death."

Jim was fine and mother prayed aloud with him, thanking God for putting the salesman at our door at exactly the right time. A worship and growth experience that came quite naturally as part of a not-so-usual day.

But when we're talking specifically about family devotions, we're talking about meaningful, planned times that will involve every child in your family in something that he will understand and find worthwhile. This is more than just reading a chapter a day aloud together. Reading alone will not teach the young child the wonders of his God. Children need to feel a part of the devotions. I'll never forget little Danny going up to his six-month-old brother Douglas and pretending, as part of the family worship, that Douglas was baby Jesus. Danny tucked the blanket around the baby as their mother held him, and then Danny told baby Jesus why he loved him.

Children need to discover that although the Bible is not a book written specifically for children, it has a message for them that they can find with the help of sensitive, guiding adults. Devotions that mean all this to your child will take a lot of thought.

Perhaps one of the first things to consider is the question, "When and how often should our family have devotions?" Obviously, for our family, Sunday before dinner was not a growth-inspiring time!

Perhaps your family might find that the only time you are all together is on Sunday afternoon. Perhaps an extended family devotional time once a week will be more effective than a few minutes' hurried worship every day of the week. Remember, daily you are a living devotional book before your child. But family devotions, per se, are an organized thing. They are important, but not half as important as the lives around which the devotional is built.

PRINCIPLES FOR DEVOTIONS

Devotions in your family are *for* your family. They are geared specifically to your child, to your family's needs. This is one reason they can have such a lasting impact. So don't let anyone give you an absolute list of how family devotions must be done. If a list of principles or a list of ideas doesn't work in your situation, drop it. It's not right for you.

Here are some principles that are important to the planning of devotions in many families. Are there any you would like to accept? Which additional ones should you add?

First, consider varying the method. You want your child to know that God sets no single pattern in which we must worship him. Rather, he leaves us with many open areas we may explore as we show our love to him.

And, of course, I think devotions can often be creative. If a child sees his parent is only interested in shoveling as much Christ-message into him as possible without giving any thought to the application behind the content, the child may lose interest. For him, there is no immediate purpose in religious training.

"My mother was reading through three chapters a day," Robert said. "I would just think about something else until the reading was done and I could escape. One day just for fun, I interrupted her reading of Noah to ask 'Did Noah take a taxi down from the mountain?' She started to explain why there were no taxis and was several sentences into it when she realized that I was kidding."

The child must see more than formal reading of a black or red book and a long, impersonal prayer when he thinks of devotions, if he is to develop the proper attitude toward God in his home. Because he is afraid of being disciplined, a child might sit still through devotions, but no parent can make the child's mind follow what is happening if he is not interested.

But what will happen if you can help your child get excited and involved? He will surely grow in the Lord and in his ability to express himself to the Lord.

Devotions must usually be planned. You might want to spend a single night or an entire month on a single topic. Set aside a special time. Some families prefer having daily devotions and extended devotions with group participation only once a week or less. Others limit devotions to prayer and a short talk-together before bedtime. Still others may elect to have family devotions just once a week. Whatever the time schedule, it should be established, and then as much as possible, adhered to.

Remember that family devotions are planned for the child more than for the parent. The main thrust should not be for you to discover new truths about God, but an opportunity for you to teach known truths to your children. Christian adults should have their private devotions on their own level of development, apart from the children.

Each child should be taught to expand the family's devotional time into private devotions just as soon as he is old enough to read and worship with meaning by himself. "I'm not coming to Sunday school today," one of my high school students told me, his teacher. "It's been a hectic couple of weeks and I haven't had time to be alone with God. I need time alone with him today, more than I need to be with the group. So I'll see you next Sunday."

This time alone with the Lord shouldn't be forced to the point that it becomes a drudgery. However, any friendship involves a lot of hard work—including friendships with God. We want our children to feel their need for communion with God without feeling regimented into it. A "must" attitude placed on the child may cause him to have guilt feelings if he should miss this devotional time. Worship then becomes a psychological ritual done as a service to God. This attitude is not only harmful to the child's spiritual growth, it is also not biblical. Becoming a growing Christian is hard work. True, and it is also exciting.

Ask yourself about family devotions, "How can I get my child actively involved?" The child should become a participant in the devotional period, not just a listener who is going to get all this godly information through the ear-gate alone.

Although many devotional periods will be structured, they should not follow a rigid pattern that can't be broken, should a more relevant problem come into prominence.

In an ideal situation family devotions should be a parent project—both parents. Mother and father should work together to teach about God.

WILL THESE IDEAS HELP YOUR FAMILY GET STARTED?

Devotions should be fun because they represent to your child one of the most important aspects of his spiritual maturity. No book is going to give all the aid you need. The following devotional ideas are just that—ideas. They are not complete in themselves. Rather they should be expanded by you into something that can be tried in your home. These suggestions can be an incentive. They can help you put before your child exciting worship experiences with his God.

Children of all ages need to feel included in each devotional time. For this reason, the following devotionals offer ideas for each child within a given structure.

You don't want your child to feel that family devotions are boring or a waste of time. He should be allowed to progress at his own speed and to his own depth.

Devotions are for each child; each child must get from them something very personal to him.

DEVOTIONAL CAR TRIP

Aim: To emphasize to my children that although God is everywhere, he is also right here with them.

Importance of this aim: Children are faced with many fears: darkness, loneliness, newness, unhappiness. They need to know that no matter what the situation, no matter where they are, God is always with them. He loves them and he will take care of them.

Time: A full afternoon

Preparation: Before you can teach this lesson to your children, you must have already appropriated it into your own life. God the Holy Spirit lives within. He is omnipresent. There is nothing beyond his sphere of interest. You might meditate over Psalm 139 during your devotions—a preparation time for adults. Children, too, need preparation. Questions on the night before your trip might stimulate their interest. Example: Why do we sometimes worry even though we know God is always with us? Can you remember times when you felt as if God wasn't really with you? When were they? What do you suppose made you feel that way? The story booklet, ''The Little Boy Who Lost His Name'' (by Theresa Worman. Chicago: Moody Bible Institute) would be excellent pre-trip reading for the child.

The Trip: This trip has been divided into five major areas.

Although the child should know that every place the family will go, God is, he should not be given the impression that he will actually see God.

1. In the car. God's protection—you might begin a discussion on God's care of all of you when you are driving, even at times when you aren't actually thinking about God.

Children might list areas of their lives that could be dangerous if God weren't there to protect them. Examples: Walking to school; swimming in the ocean.

Very young children—work with them as they talk through a prayer. You write as they dictate, remembering to thank the Lord for his protection.

Young elementary children—have them discuss with you: Does God always protect us when we do foolish things like going over the speed limit in our cars? Why do some bad things happen to Christians, if God is able to take care of us?

2. In the country. Before the trip, select a spot in a wooded area where your family can go beyond the sight of others to talk about and feel close to God.

The entire family could try to find one living thing that God has made in the woods. This might be a worm, ants, bugs, and as the family sits and silently watches the activity of these little creatures, ask your children to be thinking of the ways God cares for other animals they have seen.

Very young children—lie down on the ground and look straight into the sky at a cloud. Children could suggest what animals the formations bring to mind. They might then discuss how God takes care of that animal. Where does it live? What does it eat? Etc.

Young elementary children—your discussion could go something like this, "Isn't it wonderful how God made everything different? Let's collect some of these things that God has made for a seasonal display that we will arrange at home. God must have loved us very much to create all these things we enjoy. Do you think God just gave us all this and then left the world? No, his hand is still on everything and he is here with us."

When your children get home with the things they have collected, why not do pencil rubbings with leaves and other objects that will lie flat? It's a great way to save your devotional trip. Arrange your materials in a nice design no bigger than the size of your hand. Cover the design with a thin sheet of white paper. Rub over your design on the white paper with a soft lead pencil or pencil crayon. Press firmly and evenly on the sides of the pencil, not the point. Put the rubbings on display. Perhaps add a Bible verse about God's care. Leave the verse and the rubbings on display until everyone in the family has learned the verse.

3. As we play. In an open area, plan some games with your children that you wouldn't ordinarily play at home. For example, have a peanut scramble or a treasure hunt for such things as a four-leaf clover, forked stick, pink flower.

In the middle of the play, stop and thank God for being with you when you are having a good time, doing things that are both fun and good for growing bodies.

4. From a hill. Do you live in an area where there is some lookout point, observation tower, or hill from which the children can view the countryside? You might sit, rest, and have a snack there.

Questions for conversation during this quiet time could be: Why do you suppose God made so many different things in the world? What is the most beautiful thing in the world to you? How can you be sure God made it? If God loves us so much, why didn't he make all the world as beautiful as it is here?

Your children might enjoy putting their praise into an original poem or song.

5. In a city or town. Find a contrast to your wooded experience in the factories, buildings, and crowds of people. In the larger cities there are observation decks that would work beautifully for this part of your trip.

Discussion could follow these lines: "There must be (hundreds, thousands) of people out there and most of them do not love Jesus. When God has given us so many things, how do you suppose that makes him feel?

Why do you think people don't always want to love God?"

The family could list things they could do that would help some of those people learn of God, who is with Christians all the time. (Children should be aided in thinking of those close to them, perhaps children in their neighborhood or school class they could invite to church or a Bible club in your home. Don't forget the simple things in family life—children could share with their friends why they took this trip. Don't forget the more difficult task of living as a family that loves each other and loves God. Even very young playmates can tell when there is something special about a family.

6. An ending. You could end the outing with sentence prayers that would thank the Lord for always being with each of you no matter where you are or what you are doing.

AROUND THE WORLD WE WORSHIP

Aim: To teach your family about children of other races and cultures who worship the same God, only in different languages or surroundings, and to instill in your children a feeling of oneness for those Christians who are different from them.

Importance of this aim: This is the age when prejudices are being formed, when children discover that everyone isn't quite like they are. If they can understand when they are young that difference doesn't mean inferiority, they will have learned a valuable lesson. They should know that people of every description can worship God and that Christianity as they know it in our culture is no better than the Christianity of others whose skins or habits are just a bit different.

Time: This topic could be spread over a full month. Suggestions for three weeks are given here. Perhaps the family could work out the final week's devotions around a country or group of people in which your church has a particular interest.

Preparation: Each week your home bulletin board could be decorated with pictures of the country to be "visited." Perhaps different organizations in your area would have pictures, curios, or costumes they could lend or show during this event.

1. Alaska. Your children could make an Alaskan atmosphere by covering a window with snowflakes they have made by folding tissue paper and cutting it into different shapes.

Discussion suggestion: "If you were an Alaskan child, what do you think would be some of the areas in which you would ask God for special help? In what ways are your answers a lot like the things *you* ask God for help with?"

Pretend time: We are Alaskan children and have heard little about Jesus. You have come to tell us about him. What story would you choose from the Bible to tell boys and girls who know little about Jesus' love? (The children could take turns being the Christian adult and telling the story to the Alaskan children—the rest of the family. Primary or junior children might also like to tell why they chose this particular story.)

Pray for these children.

Since a lesson, to really mean anything to the young child, must have carryover into his own life, you will want to work on a project through the week that is connected with the country you studied during devotions.

Example: Ask a missionary to arrange a pen-pal for the primary-junior child—or perhaps just a postcard exchange with a child in Alaska. Repair and pack warm clothing to be sent to a country that has difficult winters.

The children might start a month's prayer request list, which for the younger child could be a picture list of things the child wants to pray for in connection with the group of people he has been studying.

If you have a large world map, spread it out on the floor and find the country or state you will be praying for. For very young children this will have little meaning, but third grade children and older will enjoy this activity.

Older children might want to make a compass that

would, after a mighty long walk, bring them to the countries
or state they are discussing. You'll need: needle, cork,
knife, bowl, magnet, water. Cut a disk about a half inch
off the end of the cork. Make a narrow slice in the top of
the disk just big enough to fit the needle in the slice.
Magnetize the needle. Stroke it twenty times in one
direction on one leg of the magnet. After each stroke,
raise the needle in a small semicircle above the magnet
before the next stroke. Now place the needle into the slice
on the cork so the needle floats horizontally. When you
put the cork into the bowl of water, the magnetized
needle will always point in a north-south direction. Try
a walk through your house to find the northernmost point.
Perhaps you could have your prayer time for
youngsters in Alaska at this point in your house.

Another activity could be making aluminum foil
murals of people in the countries you will be studying.
Aluminum foil is easy to squeeze into shape. Start by
tearing a square. In the center of the square place a round
wad of paper and twist the tin foil around that wad. It
will become the head. From then on it's easy to make arms
and legs and bodies. Older children will want to look in
resource books to see how they can make the people from
the place they are studying look as authentic as
possible. They might even want to draw backgrounds that
look like the special place and put their tin foil figures in
front of them.

2. Russia. In a dark room lighted with a single candle,
the family might learn a little of what it would be like not to
have freedom of worship. The children should
understand that it's very difficult for children to learn
about God in Russia because there are no Sunday
schools. Often the people are afraid of the government.
Sometimes parents are afraid to tell their children Bible
stories for fear the children will tell someone who will
report on the family. Christians cannot freely read their
Bibles. And often, because they have so few Bibles, they
tear out pages and pass them around. Some people have
never owned a whole Bible.

Discussion: In what ways are we more fortunate than

Russian boys and girls who love Jesus? What things do you think Russian Christians could teach us? Why do you think God sometimes allows people who don't love him to keep children from hearing and worshiping our true God at church?

Pretend time: We are in an underground meeting and have no Bibles. If we did we couldn't read them because we dare not turn on the lights. Let's go around the family circle and see how many Bible verses we remember. If you wish, you may tell a Bible story instead. (Following this, you might like to read a Bible story from a Bible story book to show children how lucky they are to have all the stories of the Bible to read.)

Pray for children in countries where Christians are not free. Thank God for the freedom your family has.

Decide on a project that might help children who can't worship freely hear about God. The children might want to make a personal contribution to a radio station that beams the message of Christ into Communist countries. The family might want to make a contribution to Radio Free Europe to help sustain freedom.

Beginner children could draw a picture thanking God that they have a Bible story book they can look at, that they don't have to hide.

Early elementary children might write a poem that you could set to music and sing as your family's thanks to God for the freedom you have.

3. Family of a different race (or place). Would it be possible to invite a family of a different race into your home for an evening? It might be the beginning of a long friendship. And if you have young children who may not have seen people with a different color skin, you can help them gain the right perspective on color.

Ideally, both families should have children about the same age and both should be aware of the purpose of this devotional period. The theme should not be integration, but rather the fostering of love and understanding that comes from a right perspective and deeper knowledge of the "different."

Very small children don't seem to notice skin colors. I heard this story told by the mother of a small boy who had discovered a playmate of a different color. She knew this was a new experience for her son, so when he came in she said, "Did you see anything different about Joseph?" "Oh, yes," her son answered. "He could throw a ball farther than anybody but daddy." But how soon many Christians are willing to forget how far someone can throw a ball and remember only that "He's not quite right, he's unlike me."

Discussion among the two families: Children who have not been exposed to people of different colors may have some very personal questions they would like to ask. They should be allowed to if they think of the questions without suggestion from grownups. For instance: What makes our skins look different? What does yours feel like? This is a get-acquainted time.

I spent three years teaching in a missionary school in Japan. Compared to many Japanese adults, I am enormous, so you can imagine how huge I looked to small children when I visited in towns where few Occidental people came. More than once I have heard the racing of little feet behind me and almost felt the jump as little boys tried to see if they could jump up high enough to reach above my head. Great fun for them, and it didn't hurt me at all to smile and invite those who didn't make it to try again. They were finding out that I was different—very, very tall! But they were also finding out that I smiled and I was nice.

You might use a story that builds an attitude of understanding between people who look different and have the same Savior. I found one story in which Jewish and Samaritan boys discover by accident that, in spite of the traditions of hate, they can love and have a good time with each other. Consider having your children play the stories you find.

Since there are special guests this evening, the family might plan refreshments, perhaps a combination of the favorite treats both families of children enjoy.

Pray for each other. Perhaps the adults could pray for friendships among all Christians. The children could thank God for their new friends.

After the evening, young children might exchange pictures they have drawn of each other. These pictures could be placed in a real frame and be added to the children's valued possessions.

Depending on the logistics, it might not be possible for the two families to see each other often. Primary children might enjoy a postcard pen-pal. Or the children could agree to send each other postcards from day or vacation trips.

You might make plans for an exchange visit. Ken invited us to visit his home and attend the Greek festival at his church. He and his two preschool children spoke English, but his wife spoke very little. What fun! She and I acted out what we wanted to say to each other and the children would grin and translate if either of us was too far away from the intended meaning of the other. We ate our festival meal with another Greek couple. "I think Greek women are the most beautiful in the world." one woman said. "I sure hope my son doesn't marry an outsider." She caught herself, looked at me, and we both laughed. Sharing each other's food, each other's prejudices, and each other's language: how much we have to give to each other if we would dare.

WORSHIP THROUGH MUSIC

Aim: To teach our children to be more aware of their religious musical heritage and encourage them to give special attention to the words as well as the music.

Importance of this aim: Children are all too often taught the flippant choruses of the church, while great Christian music, representing some of the highest expressions of praise and worship, is overlooked. This is the time for a devotion in music appreciation. Children's singing can become genuninely worshipful.

Time: One to two hours

Preparation: You might invest in several books on the stories of great hymns. Junior-age children could prepare a short oral report on the background of a hymn to be presented during the worship time.

Example of a hymn report taken from Edward C. May's book *Family Worship Idea Book* (Concordia Publishing House): "Stand Up, Stand Up for Jesus." This hymn grew out of a tragedy in the life of Dudley A. Tyng, an evangelist. In 1858, 1000 men responded to a sermon Tyng preached on Exodus 10:11, "Go, now, ye that are men and serve the Lord." A few weeks later, Pastor Tyng died suddenly in an accident. His last words were, "Tell them to stand up for Jesus."

Rev. George Duffield preached a sermon the following Sunday and he ended it with a poem he had written around Tyng's words. It was essentially the words to the hymn, "Stand Up, Stand Up for Jesus." Later George J. Webb set the words to music, and today the words and music are inseparable.

Before your family learns a new hymn, time should be spent discussing the meaning of the hymn's words.

Children should hear a song as many as seven times before they sing it, because it's much easier to teach it correctly than try to correct faulty timing or melody. A child who can play the piano might present the new song as a special number to the group. If it is the type of song that lends itself to accompaniment on rhythm instruments, you might cut dowel wood into rhythm sticks or attach a piece of yarn to a nail which, when hit with another nail, makes a mellow and "oriental" sound.

Allow time for family prayer and praise in favorite songs.

As a carryover activity, children might want to set a poem to music or perhaps even write their own poem.

WOULD THIS WORK IN YOUR HOME?

1. Plant a missionary garden. Plant things that children would be able to sell and give the money to a special missions project. My brother and I had a moneymaking garden for several years. We would sell the gladiolus that grew there and use all the money to go swimming at the local pool. It wasn't that we wouldn't have been rather excited about a mission project. We just never thought of it.

Sometimes an idea is all that's needed to get a new and exciting summer spiritual journey started.

If the children are old enough, this project could belong totally to them—planting, weeding, and selling of produce. Keep a check on how they are doing. Be heavy on praise. But it's their project.

"I was still in elementary school," Jayne said, "when I baby-sat for a few hours one afternoon. I earned two dollars, my first earned money. I sent it to a missionary my family supported. I knew him because he had visited in our church and in our home. He was born in a foreign country and I could even correctly pronounce his difficult name.

"He wrote back in person to tell me how much that money meant to him. The whole giving experience was very positive. The patterns I set have stayed with me throughout my life."

2. A child should learn the true meaning of Christmas beyond the tinsel and bright lights. God gave his Son as a gift to people who deserved nothing because they had chosen the way of disobedience. Now through Jesus Christ, anyone can come to know God personally, because Christ made it possible for people to get rid of their sins. When the child has accepted the Christian message as his own, on the level he can understand it, he will want to do more during the holiday than receive. There are many projects that can be planned and worked through during Christmas days that will let the child put the idea of giving into practice.

Help your child sort his toys and suggest he give those in his "gift" pile to a mission that could use them or an organization working with underprivileged children. Parents may find that giving the toys to an organization is better than allowing the child to give to another child because the giver may get the idea he is better than the child who is receiving.

The gift pile could include toys that the child has outgrown and perhaps several toys that are "offering" toys. These are toys the child still likes and plays with but he wants to give away because he still has so much more than many children. Be sure the child knows that the "offering" toys he gives will not be replaced at Christmas. They are truly gifts.

Children might enjoy making cookies for senior citizen homes. They might include a letter or a picture telling what Christmas means to them. The family could visit in a home or hospital where there are people who may be lonely at Christmas. There are lots of family craft ideas that could be given to elderly people. Often these people love the gifts, not because of any monetary value or because of their beauty, but because a child made it and presented it in person.

Children might decide to invite foreign students into their home for the holidays as a witness to these visitors. All the responsibility for carrying out this idea shouldn't fall to you. Your children might agree to give up one gift so that the visitor might have several. Children should help with all the cooking and housework. They might enjoy making favors for the table and Christmas decorations. The whole family might plan a special extended-family devotion for the afternoon.

3. Art galleries often have special displays for Christian holidays—Easter and Christmas. The family could spend an hour or two at the gallery discussing why a picture is biblical in presentation, why another is not, why each person prefers one picture to another.

Children could copy one of the paintings and the representation could be used in your special home holiday display.

4. Use special family days to their devotional advantage. On his birthday, the child might like to make a list of attitudes he will try to improve with the Lord's help during the coming year. Then the rest of the family could join him in prayer.

One family I know has a personal flag for each child. On that child's birthday the flag is hung outside and the family prays for the child in a special way.

In our family, nearly everyone's birthday is on some special day—or at least near it. My father's is the fifth of July. What a perfect time to talk about what our country means to us and how we as Christians can support its laws and pray for its leaders. My brother almost hit New Year's Day with his January 2 special day. It was a good time to talk about how God had helped our family in the last year and what we were willing to do to help him in the year to come. My mother's Flag Day birthday was another opportunity to share how we feel about our nation. But my birthday—I'm not sure what we could do with that. November 1 used to be the first day of hunting season. We could thank the Lord for provisions of food and for his safety. (Safety would have made sense to us because as children we lived on a farm and my mother was always worried that some near-sighted hunter would think my brother and I were deer.) November 1 is also All Saints Day. Our family did not celebrate this day, but it would have been a good opportunity to thank God for the Christians in our past who were important to our spiritual growth. What holiday devotions could your family plan?

5. Still pictures of Bible scenes are easy for small children to make. Simple bathrobes will do for costumes. Each child would decide which scenes he could best illustrate by standing perfectly still. These still-pictures could be photographed and entered into a children's book of Bible stories that the family selected and illustrated themselves.

6. Have a special events calendar on which is printed the dates that the family will be participating in a special project. Holidays that the child celebrates as well as some special days the family might like to invent could be listed. For instance, the family could play a second Christmas in July and remember Christ's birth on that day. Children could make presents and sing Christmas carols.

This special events calendar is as much for you as for the children. Remember the vice president who started writing in family days? Actually family days are as important as guest speaker days at church. They are days that will make a difference in the lives of our children.

7. Preschool children would enjoy making a sound track for a record story. You or older children in the family could read a story while the younger child makes the background noises. A story should be picked that lends itself to this type of thing. For example, David, the musical shepherd boy; Jesus' triumphant entry to Jerusalem; the lost sheep.

8. Children could make some things with which the

child of Bible times was acquainted, such as water pots, camels from clay, clay homes. These articles made from modeling clay or play dough could form the basis for a discussion of life in Bible times. Through this study, the child will become better acquainted with the terminology and the background of Bible stories. For your older children, these small clay items could be placed on a relief map for study of geography of the land where Jesus walked.

9. National holidays could be observed during the family devotional period. Each member could make a list of problems and blessings that he would like to make a matter of specific prayer.

Because your child should learn that a Christian is part of his world and should be aware of what is going on in it, you could use part of a devotional time to write a letter to a congressman on some issue important to you.

In all probability someone will acknowledge the letter, and this will give the child a feeling of personal acquaintance with a leader of his country.

Be watching for stories that can be used in your devotional prayer time that will help you teach about the importance of becoming involved. Here are two that I wrote for children's magazines. The first is aimed at children who are in fifth through eighth grade. The second would be understood by children from third grade through sixth grade.

THEY
A Parable About Caring

Cary always got upset when she flew over the river. "They ought to do something," she would coo and flap her wings in protest. "Look at that junk cluttering the riverbank. See that candy wrapper floating downstream? What a mess. They really ought to do something."

Cary was a State House pigeon. In fact, she called the ledge outside the governor's office her home.

That afternoon she shared with her friends what she'd seen.

"Things are bad all over," Fleck, a speckled brown and white pigeon agreed. "Remember when the air used to be clear?" He stuck his beak into the air.

"Yeah. They ought to do something."

"And when I was a little squab, I can remember people sitting on the steps of the State House feeding us corn," said another pigeon. "Now they trick us with Styrofoam."

"People sure are dirty birds. They could kill us with junk like that."

"Someone should do something to stop them."

"And those homes over there," the conversation continued. "Their paint is peeling and their windows are broken."

"They ought to do something."

"Look at that kid down there sticking his gum on the side of the State House. I've a good mind to dive at him. That would keep him from being so sloppy with state property," Cary said.

"Why bother?" Fleck said. "He'd just chew it for a few more blocks and stick it somewhere else. I don't think there's anything they can do about it. They don't know how to train kids nowadays."

Throughout the conversation, an older, slate-gray pigeon had stood on the ledge listening.

"Who's they?" he asked.

Cary cooed on. "Why don't we form ourselves into a flying protest poster? We could get thousands of pigeons from the city and maybe import a few from the countryside. We could spell out the words, 'They ought to do something,' and fly over the city in formation. Boy, they would do something then."

"Who's they?" the gray pigeon asked again.

Suddenly the window behind them opened. The pigeons were used to the governor, so they only fluttered a few feet.

The governor stood at the window and looked out over the city. "Crime, pollution, broken families, uncaring people. It's awful."

The pigeons turned to look at him. He was almost always talking—that's what governors did. But he rarely talked when there was no one around.

The governor sighed and turned back toward his desk, but not before the pigeons heard him say, "I wish they'd do something."

"Who's they?" the gray pigeon cooed.

Cary bobbed her head from side to side. "Well, that's a good question." She pecked at one of her feathers. "I'm sure I don't know, but if we could ever find them and let them know all that needs to be done around here, they could certainly make a difference in this country."

What discussion questions might you use? Of course, you would gear them to your specific situation, but you might try some like these: Who are "they"? What things need to be done in our neighborhood? Do you think a Christian should be more interested in keeping our neighborhood and country clean and healthy than someone who doesn't know Jesus? What things could our family do?

What sections in the Bible might you study? Genesis is always excellent. Look at the world as God created it and contrast what you see with what he intended. Or, if your children are young teens, you might have them compare portions from the first few chapters in Isaiah with our country. What does God expect from his people?

The Beginning of a Politician

"And what do you want to be when you grow up?" Mrs. Cramer asked Karen.

A couple of months ago Karen would have had some smart remark to shoot back. "Oh, a digger of very straight ditches." Or, "A monkey for a near-sighted organ grinder." But now, for the first time, she didn't think the question was silly; now she knew the answer.

"A politician," she answered.

Karen could remember the exact evening when the seeds of her decision had begun to grow. She was stretched out across the family room floor watching TV and eating licorice strings. The show had a lot of funny spots, but as the half hour passed, Karen began to feel uneasy about watching it. In one scene, the lead character fell asleep in church and started snoring. There were jokes about God and about the money people gave to the church. For the first time in her life, Karen switched off the TV before the show ended, and she was proud of herself for doing it.

"How could I sit there and let her make fun of my God and his house?" she asked her neighbor Raymond the next day.

"Big deal!" Raymond was the sarcastic type. "So one person switches off her TV. That's not going to make any difference."

"So you switch off yours too," Karen said. "And I'll mention it at club meeting this week and at Sunday school. We'll start a switch-off strike, and everyone who feels what we're doing is right can pass the word."

"Hey, you really feel strongly about this, don't you?"

"You bet! It might not make a whole lot of difference, but God's sure never going to tell me I didn't try."

Raymond nodded. "Why don't you write to the company that advertises on the program and let the people there know what you're doing? It's only fair. After all, if their sales are going to hit bottom 'cause no one sees their advertisements, they ought to know why. Maybe they'll switch to a program we feel good about watching."

Raymond and Karen passed the word, and a lot of their Christian friends agreed the plan was a good one. Of course, as the weeks passed, Karen and Raymond had no way of checking to see which kids continued to switch off the program, but they kept their promise to God and felt good about it.

One Friday afternoon as they were walking home from school, Karen picked up a soft drink can in the gutter. "I'll bet I can hit that old barrel in the vacant lot," she told Raymond.

He shrugged and she threw.

Bull's eye!

"Big deal." It was one of his favorite phrases. "So now you've added to the junk in there. What do you want? A flip-top medal?"

"I wonder why someone doesn't build something there," Karen said. "It's a good spot."

"My dad says Show More Auto Parts bought it, but when auto sales went into a slump, they put off building another store here. Sandra Patton's father is the manager of their store on Brooker Street."

"It's a shame to see the lot turn into the neighborhood garbage can."

"Oh, listen to the girl," Raymond mocked. "Just as if you never had anything to do with the mess."

"So now I'm going to have something to do with cleaning it up," Karen said. "I read once where a bunch of kids made a 'pocket park' out of a lot. They cleaned it up and even got some companies to donate play equipment for the little kids."

Raymond looked impressed. "We could go talk to Mr. Patton tomorrow morning. Since Sandra's in our class, he'd probably listen to us. If he said yes, we could get started tomorrow afternoon. I think lots of kids would help."

The next morning as Raymond and Karen told the Show More Manager what they wanted to do, he seemed pleased.

"Two nights ago kids about your age threw rocks at my windows," he said. "When the police caught them, they said they did it just to hear the glass break. I was disgusted. You two have made me feel better about kids. Sure, go ahead. Clean off that lot. We won't be doing anything with it for at least another year."

Karen and Raymond had just turned to leave when she got another idea. "Mr. Patton," she said, "once we get it cleaned, it would be nice to have some playthings like a sliding board and a jungle gym. How would your company like to donate them? We would paint a sign with your company's name on it and put it on the lot. That way when you build, people in the neighborhood would already know your name and like you because you did something nice for their kids."

"Yeah," Raymond added. "It's good business."

Mr. Patton laughed and nodded. "OK, it's yours. Let me know when you've done your part and I'll have something delivered." He turned to Karen. "Young lady, you're quite a politician."

The project took much longer than Karen and Raymond thought it would, and throughout the Saturdays that followed, more than kids got involved. Mothers and fathers hauled carloads of junk away. The local hardware store donated twelve pairs of working gloves so the kids' hands wouldn't be cut by sharp objects on the lot. The gas station down the street volunteered refueling services—free Cokes to the kids working on the project.

Karen and Raymond, along with their friends, boxed and bagged the junk. They raked the lot to get rid of stones that might hurt small children. With donated lumber and the help of a neighborhood couple who liked to work with wood, they built a fence around the area. They decided where to put the play things for the little kids and where the older kids could play volleyball or soccer.

One Saturday afternoon Karen was sitting in the middle of a sandpile that had been dumped for children to play in. She had a board on her lap and colored paints on her left. She was almost finished with the sign that would read, "Play Equipment Given by Show More Auto Parts," when a man walked through the pocket park gate and over to her. "You kids have done great things here," he said.

"In the spring, we'll plant flowers around the fence," Karen said. "You should have seen the mess before we got started."

"I did," the man said. "I'm only sorry I didn't think of cleaning it off. I probably would have gotten every vote in the neighborhood."

Karen looked at the man again. "I've seen your picture in the paper, haven't I?"

"I hope the rest of the world has that good a memory. I'm Joseph Majorivitz. I'm running for councilman in this district. What's your name?"

"Karen Fitzwilliams."

"Hey, I'm talking to the big wheel of this project, aren't I?" Mr. Majorivitz laughed. "Mr. Patton down at the auto parts store mentioned you. His daughter told him you were also the head of a campaign to stop people from watching a TV program you didn't approve of. You've got tremendous talent for organizing things and getting them moving. I'm glad you're not old enough to run against me. I might lose."

"Mr. Patton told me I would make a good politician," Karen said. "I think I would like helping people. There are a lot of things that need to be done around here."

"Why don't you come to my campaign headquarters and help me?" Mr. Majorivitz said. "My people can give you some papers to read that will tell you what I want to do in this district. If you think I'd make a good councilman, help me work. Frankly, lady, I'd rather have you on my side than against me."

Karen and Mr. Majorivitz laughed and she agreed to come. She watched him as he walked away. He was friendly, and he was interested in the community. He had remembered her name. That probably meant that he was smart and that he cared about people. He had a lot of talents she'd need to develop before she could become a good politician.

Yes, thought Karen, I have a lot to learn, and it's time I got started.

Wednesday she picked up the materials and read them. What he said made sense. Most of his projects were things that didn't take a lot of money, but would involve work. "He's a good writer," Karen told her father. "I could understand what he meant. I was thinking about becoming a politician someday, but it's hard. I'd have to learn to be a good writer and public speaker. Maybe I'll never be good enough."

"You've already begun developing some skills a politician needs," her father said. "And you've got a number of years to polish those talents. I'm sure as you continue to develop, God will give you opportunities to use the gifts he gave you."

"Do you think I could help Mr. Majorivitz win?" Karen asked.

"I don't know what he'd have for you to do, but it wouldn't hurt to try. It would be good experience for a person who may someday be a politician."

The next day she went back to campaign headquarters hoping that Mr. Majorivitz would be there. Instead there was a woman typing addresses on envelopes. She looked tired.

"Do you have something I could do?" Karen asked. "I'd really like to help Mr. Majorivitz win."

The woman looked surprised. "Well, we have a man coming in this evening to stuff information into these envelopes I'm addressing. No, I don't thing there's anything. You're a little too young."

Karen pressed her lips together. No, I'm not, she thought. "Are those envelopes you're typing going to be stuffed with information about Mr. Majorivitz?" she asked.

"Yes."

"How do you know people will open them? My mom often throws away junk mail because she's sure without even opening it that she isn't interested."

"Well, we're doing what we can." The woman looked annoyed.

"But," Karen continued, "she always opens letters that are addressed by hand. I could write some of those addresses you haven't done yet."

For the first time, the woman looked interested. "Good idea," she said. "In fact, a very good idea." She gave Karen a sheet of names and a stack of envelopes.

From then on until election night, Karen addressed envelopes in her free time. Mr. Majorivitz was in and out of the office. Sometimes he had time to talk, but often he would just smile and rush on to his next appointment.

On election day, Karen and her parents were invited to a Wait-Until-the-Vote-Is-Counted party. The party was fun and a little scary. As the radio announced the vote, the room would get quiet. If Mr. Majorivitz was ahead, everyone would cheer. If he was behind, they would shoot encouraging remarks across the room.

But as the evening got later, there was less cheering. Finally everyone realized that, in spite of all their work, Mr. Majorivitz had lost the election.

Mr. Majorivitz stood up and got everyone's attention. "Thank you all for your hours and your belief in me. We've done our best. Now it's our responsibility to work with the new councilman, without bitterness, to make this district a safer, better place to live."

After his speech, people began to quietly leave. Karen liked the way he tried to say good-bye to everyone and give personal thanks for what each had done. When it came her turn, she felt more sad than she had ever felt before.

"Thanks, Karen," he said. "You were my youngest and perhaps one of my best helpers. There will be other elections and maybe we'll work together again."

"But you were the better candidate," she said. "Why didn't you win?"

"Maybe people didn't know me well enough. But don't ever not do something because you're afraid you'll lose," he said. "Remember. If you do your best job, you'll force your opponent to do an even better job to beat you. That's one of the things that's so great about elections. It forces everyone to do his best. Understand?"

Karen nodded and smiled what she knew was a pretty sad-looking smile.

"Remember what I said," Mr. Majorivitz said. "It may come in handy the first time you run for governor."

What questions might you discuss? Here are some of my ideas: What are some of the things we know about the people who lead our city? (You might want to drive past their offices and homes.) What people in the Bible were leaders in politics? (You might consider Joseph in Egypt or King David or Pilate.) What made these rulers good? Bad? What are some things we should pray for concerning our leaders? How could our family help a leader we really believe in?

10. After hearing a Bible story during devotions, your child might think through the story in terms of how it might have happened if the same story had been set in the modern world. For example: In the story of Naaman's maid, the little girl might have been adopted. Her new father got very sick; she explained the power of prayer to him, and for the first time, he believed in God. Then because it is God's will, he gets well. The child, after he has talked through the modern story, could draw flash card pictures to illustrate; or draw simple backgrounds on flannel to which

figures backed with flannel would adhere. He could then share his modern story. Pictures might be cut from magazines and catalogs.

This modern-day activity will help you know that your child really does understand some of the lessons in the Bible story. In a way, you are asking him to do an age-level paraphrase.

A QUICK RESTATEMENT

Every child has within him some creative potential. Your child has within him or her some creative potential! There is no exception. Although some degree of creativeness, originality, or inventiveness is innate to your child, the responsibility for the development of this uniqueness in the child will fall to a large extent on you.

To raise a child creatively is not an easy task, for it will mean training him to be different, to go against tradition and mediocrity. But as the child's life is changed by the creative thinking he is stimulated to do at home, so will he be changed by what he sees in your lives—the lives of his parents. From your example he will see life as an exciting adventure to be lived fully. His early introduction to the possibilities which lie within him will affect his attitude toward himself, his relations with others, and his adoration and worship of his God.

Your most important job is to raise a human being. This young individual, before he can work in the world, must learn his part in its operation. He must have a good self-concept, actually loving himself because he knows that God loves him. If he accepts himself as he is he will go on to do the very best job possible with what he has available to him. Because he knows himself and is not afraid to face life as it really is, he will not be afraid to give himself to others, to share with them, to accept them just the way they are. As the creative person continues his self-expansion, his path away from the ordinary, he will be better able to present an extraordinary Christ to others.

The ability to be creative is a gift from God, and, as is true of gifts in every area, Christians must use their creativity to bring glory to God. How wonderful when our creations point to and glorify God!

Because your child has found beauty and expression, he will no longer be at home in the clichés and traditions that would limit his relationship with Christ. He will want to know God more personally in terms that mean something special to him. He will want to give God not simply a parroted love dutifully offered. He will give instead a real devotion that comes from deep within himself, as he works within the limits given in Holy Scripture, to present before his God his personal and unique outpouring of worship.